JEWISH ENCOUNTERS

Jonathan Rosen, General Editor

Jewish Encounters is a collaboration between Schocken and Nextbook, a project devoted to the promotion of Jewish literature, culture, and ideas.

>nextbook

PUBLISHED

FORTHCOMING

Rashi

ELIE WIESEL

RASHI

A PORTRAIT

Translated from the French by
Catherine Temerson

NEXTBOOK · SCHOCKEN · NEW YORK

Schocken Books and colophon are registered
trademarks of Random House, Inc.

This translation is based on an unpublished French work
by Elie Wiesel, copyright © by Elirion Associates, Inc.

Library of Congress Cataloging-in-Publication Data
Wiesel, Elie, [date]
Rashi / Elie Wiesel ; translated from the French
by Catherine Temerson.
p.   cm.
Includes bibliographical references and index.
ISBN 978-0-8052-4254-6 (alk. paper)
1. Rashi, 1040–1105.   2. Rashi, 1040–1105. Perush Rashi 'al
ha-Torah.   3. Jewish scholars—France—Troyes—Biography.
4. Rabbis—France—Troyes—Biography.
5. Troyes (France)—Biography.   I. Title.
BM755.S6W54 2009
296.1092—dc22
[B]   2009009930

www.schocken.com

Printed in the United States of America

First Edition

2 4 6 8 9 7 5 3 1

For Elijah and Shira
from their grandfather

WHEN THEY GROW UP
THEY WILL STUDY THE GREAT WORK
OF OUR ADMIRABLE ANCESTOR.

CONTENTS

PREFACE

Why Rashi?

And why me?

For centuries, others—many others—in lots of different countries, have written about his life and work in their native or sacred tongues. Why should I add my own analysis and my own commentary to these?

I could almost invoke our personal, not to say private, ties. But so could others, indeed some do, and they do so well. Did they hear from their parents that they had their place in a genealogy that could be traced back to the illustrious Rabbi Shlomo, son of Yitzhak? Mine referred to this often. I was not supposed to forget that I was the descendant of Rabbi Yeshayahu ben Abraham Horovitz ha-Levi, the author of *Shnei Luchot ha-Brit* and the *Shla ha-Kadosh* whose brilliant depth haunted my adolescence, and of his contemporary, Rabbi Yom Tov Lipmann ha-Levi, the author of *Tosafot Yom Tov*, whose dramatic life and erudite work on the Talmud and its commentaries are indispensable to anyone who devotes himself to the study of ancient texts.

According to tradition, the two great Teachers were descendants of Rashi.

Is that the real reason for my doing this? To state publicly what my understandably proud parents told me in private as a way of impressing my obligations? I don't think so. If, at my age, I decided to say yes to Jonathan Rosen and interrupt my work in progress to sketch this portrait of Rashi, it is because I feel the need to tell him everything I owe to him.

I think of Rashi and I feel overwhelmed by a strange nostalgia: my reaction appears to be both intellectual and emotional. And why not say it? I discover I am sentimental.

Ever since childhood, he has accompanied me with his insights and charm. Ever since my first Bible lessons in the heder, I have turned to Rashi in order to grasp the meaning of a verse or word that seemed obscure.

He is my first destination. My first aid. The first friend whose assistance is invaluable to us, not to say indispensable, if we've set our heart on pursuing a thought through unfamiliar subterranean passageways, to its distant origins. A veiled reference from him, like a smile, and everything lights up and becomes clearer.

Of course, it is the Jewish child in me who thanks him. But Rashi's appeal is addressed to everyone. What I mean is this: his passion for delving into a text in order to find a hidden meaning passed on by generations can move, interest, and enrich all those whose life is governed by learning.

His voice comes to us from afar, from a great distance in time and space, but it allows us to never turn our back on the goal and never go astray along the way.

Rashi

1

Impressions

I stroll around the new and old streets of the city of Troyes, in Champagne. It still vibrates with medieval history. I am shown the Hôtel-Dieu at the corner of the rue de la Cité and the quai des Comptes: this is where the *Porte de la Juiverie*, the old gateway to the Jewish neighborhood, was located. And what about the fairs where the Jews from the nearby cities met to discuss business and the rules of ritual? As always, these are to be found in books.

Cited by Irving Agus and again by Gérard Nahon, the Hebraic name of Troyes (or Troyias) first appears in a document written by Yosef bar Shmuel Tov-elem of Limoges in the eleventh century: "Concerning our brothers in Rheims who used to go to the fair in Troyes and whom an enemy lord captured (or persecuted)."

Who were these Jews? What enemy is he referring to? We know there used to be a synagogue here (there is even a street named after it), and there used to be a street of the Jews, a *rue des Juifs* (now gone as well). There were rabbis, hence students. There were leaders, Jewish families loyal to the Law of Moses, who fought against the outside enemy and the poverty in their midst, helped the poor, and did everything they could to pay the ransom and free their co-religionists when they were taken as hostages. In spite of distances, there were deep contacts between the communities: their right to intervene in one another's affairs was recognized by the competent rabbinical authorities. After all, didn't they share a common destiny?

As for me, today, I am looking for the traces of a man whose learning still influences my life, as it does the lives of all those who have a thirst for study.

Houses, large and small, stores, gardens. The man I am looking for must have walked here, dreamed here, shed tears here over the destruction of the Temple in Jerusalem, comforted broken hearts, counseled those who had gone astray, taught them to overcome fear and hope for the arrival of the Messiah.

I remember: as a child, his cursive script frightened me; more than that of the Bible, it suggested a world that was doubtless complex and probably mysterious, where only adults had the right and competence to enter.

Later, with the years, in the heder or yeshiva, before the candles on the table, every time someone asked, "What does Rashi say?" I rushed to look at his countless commentaries. Whenever I couldn't grasp the meaning of a word, it was he, the Teacher of my Teachers, who rescued me. An intimate relationship, from child to elderly man, person to person. He said to me, as if confidentially: look, my child; fear nothing, everything must be grasped and conveyed with simplicity. Strange words stand in the way like obstacles? Start all over again with me. It happened to me too. I started all over again. You just have to break through the shell of a word, a sentence, an expression. Everything is inside them. Everything is waiting for you.

Thanks to his life, his erudition, his work, his generosity, he remains the spring from which we all drink. Without him, my thirst would never have been quenched. Without him, I would have gone astray more than once in the gigantic labyrinth that is the Babylonian Talmud.

Yet he doesn't try to impress us with his learning, his vast religious and secular culture, his originality, or even his inventive mind. He confines himself to quoting the ancients or his precursors, sometimes his peers, and even his own disciples.

Rashi or the celebration of commentary? Better yet: Rashi or the celebration of memory, and of fraternity too. The danger lies in oblivion. Were I to forget where I come from, my life would become barren and sterile. Were I to forget whom I am the descendant of, I would be doomed to despair.

I loved him. I couldn't make headway without him. Of course, I explored other approaches, other commentaries:

those of Abrabanel, Sforno, Radak, Or ha-Hayim, Ibn Ezra, but Rashi's are unique, different, indispensable. He radiates warmth and friendship. And simplicity. He is great because he remains faithful to the text, and to its literal meaning. He never uses his learning to make things complicated but to simplify. He never flaunts his erudition to impress students with the originality of his reasoning. Reconciling two words, two sentences, two verses is enough for him. To those who are timid he seems to be saying, Don't be afraid, I am here by your side.

Sometimes, in my small town, it seemed to me that Rashi had been sent to earth primarily to help Jewish children overcome loneliness.

And fear.

Under a cloudless blue sky, alone with my thoughts, and my nostalgia, I wander through the back streets of Troyes.

Where was his house? No one can tell me. His vineyard? Again, no one knows. His grave in the Jewish cemetery? His parents' graves or his wife's? The graves of his three daughters? Are there any remains of his house or his school?

I find none.

I try to use my imagination.

The father and his three daughters during the grape harvest. Their Sabbath dinners. The discussions with his students. His solitude as he bent over his worktable, consulting books and ancient documents, and writing his oeuvre whose immensity never ceases to surprise us—his commentary on the Bible and the Talmud, and his vast body of responsa, the answers he furnished to questions posed from faraway rabbis.

Yes, we need imagination in order to write about him.

In those days, the Jewish communities in the provinces along the Rhine lived between fear and hope. At times the former dominated as though attracted by unfathomable gloom, at times the latter, making the dawning sun shine bright.

Often bound to one another through religious study and commerce, they flourished at the whim or self-interest of the church authorities and political sovereigns.

At the center of the Talmudic schools, the last in the Gaonic period, was Rabbenu, our Teacher, Gershom, Meor ha-Golah, the Light of the Exile, the uncontested leader of Jewish life. In dealing with complicated questions concerning the interpretation of the Law and doubts about matters of faith, it was to him that they flocked from all over the Diaspora.

We think he died in 1040, but we're not absolutely positive. We like to think this because that was the year of Rabbi Shlomo's birth—Rabbi Shlomo, son of Yitzhak, known by his initials, Rashi. According to Rabbi Shlomo Luria, this coincidence proves the validity of the verse in Ecclesiastes, "The sun also arises, and the sun goeth down": in the world of men, as soon as a spiritual sun sets, another rises. It is simple: humanity could not survive, not even temporarily, in darkness.

Actually, other more reliable sources refer to 1028 as the date of the Gaon's death. Let us leave it up to medieval historians to decide. On the other hand, most agree on the date of Rashi's birth, 1040, and all on the date of his death, 1105.

At the time, the Jews in France lived more or less normal lives, depending on the disposition of the Church, and the mood and interest of the Capetian kings Hugh, Henry I, Philip I, Louis VI, and Louis VII. When the Jews were needed, they were left in peace. Afterward, they were disposed of.

In France, the Jewish communities considered themselves well established because they dated from ancient times. They were already there in Roman times, at first in certain specific areas, particularly near the Mediterranean coast. A *rue des Juifs* could be found everywhere and, in some cities, can still be found today: the stones are a testament to history.

Did the first Jews arrive as war prisoners with the victorious Roman legions? So it is believed. They wound up in ancient settlements like Marseilles and Narbonne. They were found scattered in other places—in Paris, Avignon,

Orléans, Metz. Protected by Roman law, they survived thanks to trade in wines and spices, travel, and what was called usury.

With the accession of the kings of Gaul, things changed. The Jews were no longer "citizens." During the sinister apocalyptic mood that prevailed around the year 1000—further inflamed by the appearance of a fiery comet in 1014 and the solar eclipse in 1033—they were unprotected. They were not even tolerated. They were singled out, here and there, and accused of causing the scourges that befell superstitious inhabitants. Forced conversions, arbitrary arrests, threats of expulsion; it seemed these invariably followed the same logic of a cruel implacable destiny. Occasionally, with a bit of luck and a lot of money, the ruler or bishop deigned to change his mind and a reprieve was granted.

The year 1017: King Robert the Pious orders the Jews to convert; when they refuse, he sets fire to synagogues and Jewish homes. In the same period, in Limoges, the Jews, loyal to their ancestral faith, are expelled. A contemporary chronicler, Adhémar de Chabanne, writes: "There were some among them who slit their own throats with their swords rather than accept baptism." In November 1012, the Jews were expelled from Mainz; in January 1013, they were back. Sometimes the Vatican itself was persuaded to intervene. Then, in 1095, in Clermont, the bloody, deadly explosion took place: Pope Urban II preached in favor of the Crusade. Destination: Palestine. The goal: to save Christianity's holy sites. Along the road, says one witness, in Rouen, the Crusaders locked the Jews in a church and ordered them to convert, then massacred them with two-edged swords, men, women, and children. Moreover, Godfrey of Bouillon declared publicly that he "wouldn't set off except if he had avenged the blood of the crucified in the blood of Israel and not let a single person with a Jewish name survive."

These atrocities, and others, were committed wherever the Crusaders of Christendom made their appearance, including in the province of Champagne, not far from Troyes.

Here and there, living in fear of the next day, the Jewish communities that were directly concerned sent messengers to their neighboring communities warning them of the imminent danger.

In most cases, they did so in vain.

However, in the area of education and culture, the situation of the Jews seems rather enviable. There was a Jewish religious culture in France well before Rashi. Several centers were well known for the distinction of their teachers. Indeed this was the period in the history of European cultural and religious thought that saw the birth of Jewish learning in France. So that as a youth Rashi knew where to go to complete his biblical and Talmudic studies. Many scholars came from Italy and settled in the Rhineland and France. Mainz, Speyer, Vitry, Worms, and Limoges attracted the best students. Among them, Shlomo, son of Yitzhak.

Who was this father? We know very little about him. Some believe he was a very erudite man. It is thought that Rashi himself asserts it. He does so by paying him a great compliment, which is this:

His impressive commentary of the Bible starts with a question asked by a Rabbi Yitzhak: why does the Bible begin with the description of the genesis of the world rather than with the first law, which concerns the calendar? We will return to this question. For the time being, let us just recall that for some exegetes, this Rabbi Yitzhak is none other than the author's father. Generally, it is believed to be a Talmudic scholar.

If this assumption is correct, it would mean that we know at least one thing about Rashi's father: he was himself a rabbi who posed questions worthy of contemplation. But beyond the fact that he was the father of one the greatest scholars of the biblical and Talmudic literature, we know very little.

Nothing more? No, not much more. We're not even sure of the basic facts of his biography. Did he have other children, a brother perhaps (just one?), who was also a *talmid hakham*, a Talmudic scholar? How old was he when he died? Was he a martyr? One source intimates as much by calling him *kadosh*, or holy, but can't this term also describe a moral life devoted to the Lord? How old was Rashi when he became an orphan? In one place, Rashi quotes him and calls his father "*Avi mori*," my father and my teacher. Does this mean he studied the Torah with him and maybe also the Babylonian Talmud? Rabbi Haim David Azulai writes that he was a true Talmudist.

Strange: we know so many things about so many individuals thanks to Rashi, and so little about the man who gave him life. And even less about his mother.

Why Rashi? The intials of Rabbi Shlomo Yitzhaki, Shlomo son of Itzhak, or, just as simply, Rabbi Shlomo she-yihyeh (may he have a long life)? The illustrious Rabbi Hayim ben Attar has his own interpretation: the name comes from the initial letters in Rabban Shel Israel, Teacher of all Israel. Rabbi Nahman of Bratzlav calls him "the brother of the Torah." The Torah and his commentary are inseparable. But the title that suits him best is simply "ha-Moreh ha-Gadol," the Great Teacher.

We don't know the precise date of his birth in 1040—or perhaps 1041. On the other hand, his date of death in 1105 is well established: the twenty-ninth day of the month of Tammuz, hence a Thursday in the middle of the summer. This date can be seen on the Parma de Rossi parchment written by one of his disciples and transcribed in 1305: "the holy ark, the holiest of holiest, the great Teacher Rabbenu Shlomo blessed in memory as righteous, son of the martyr Rabbi Yitzhak the Frenchman, was taken from us on Thursday, the twenty-ninth day of the month of Tammuz in the year 4865, aged sixty-five, and called back to the yeshiva above."

That's very scanty biographical information, is it not?

In Rashi's day, about a hundred Jewish families lived in the beautiful city of Troyes. They lived modestly and experienced no great upheavals. These occurred only in the thirteenth century. In 1288, to be exact.

It was the old story of ritual murder—stupid, ridiculous, but oh so deadly. It is mentioned in *The Lamentation of Troyes* by Yaakov ben Yehuda of Lorraine. Hate-filled fanatics put the corpse of a Christian child in the house of a Jewish notable, Isaac Chatelain. Arrested along with his whole family, interrogated, they all suffered the abuse and torture that was usual at the time. They all chose *Kiddush ha-Shem*, a martyr's death, the supreme sacrifice in the sanctification of God's name.

Dark times spawn legends of hope, dreams of a hero, which for Jews in those times meant not a soldier but a scholar, an interpreter of God's word. Several legends surround Rashi's birth. They say his parents owned a precious gem that was so luminous and sparkled so brilliantly that the Church dearly wished to acquire it for ritual use. They were offered astronomical sums and substantial benefits. Fearing both the possible temptation and the probable intimidation, they took the gem and threw it into the sea. Heaven rewarded them by giving them a son whose beneficial light was more exceptional and dazzling than that of the precious gem.

Another legend: one day Rashi's mother, in the late stage of pregnancy, was walking down a narrow, dark alley when an elegant coach coming in the opposite direction almost ran her over. A miracle occurred: she pressed her belly against the wall and the wall curved inward. They say the trace of this mysterious occurrence can still be seen today: a rounded niche in the stones.

And still another legend: fearing that he would be unable to assemble a minyan, a quorum of ten men, for his son's circumcision, Rabbi Yitzhak, the father of the future Rashi, had the surprise and joy of welcoming as his last visitor, a latecomer, the first circumcised Jew in history, the patriarch Abraham, or, according to another source, the prophet Elijah.

According to other legends, invented by hagiographers, he spoke every existing language, mastered all the sciences, religious and secular, and had journeyed to faraway lands. He was said to have visited the great poet and thinker Rabbi Yehuda ha-Levi in Spain and the Duke of Prague in his castle. He is purported to have hosted Godfrey of Bouillon, who came to consult him before leaving on the Crusade to liberate Jerusalem's holy places.

In the Hasidic literature, he is called "the holy Rashi" for his immense oeuvre was said to be inspired from the Holy Spirit, the *Shekhinah*: otherwise, as a mere human, he would never have been able to accomplish so many things in so many areas.

One Hasidic text goes so far as to imagine that Rashi did not die a natural death: that he actually never died at all but went up to heaven alive, immortal like the prophet Elijah. Which would explain why no one knows where his grave is located.

Rabbi Yitzhak Eizik of Ziditchov's commentary: When God, blessed be His Name, decided to put an end to Abraham's trials on Mount Moriah and to spare the life of his son Isaac, Abraham initially refused to hear the angel who handed down the celestial command. He gave in only when God promised him that one of Isaac's descendants would be Shlomo, son of Isaac of Troyes.

At that point Abraham had no choice.

Rashi was a precocious student, that is a fact.

We know Rashi studied—for how many years?—with his maternal uncle, Rabbi Shimon bar Yitzhak the Ancient, Rabbenu Gershom's disciple. At eighteen or twenty, he went to Mainz in Germany to study at the yeshiva founded by the aforementioned Rabbenu Gershom, where under the latter's authority, several great Sages assisted the students. In this way, the young Rashi had access to Talmudic manuscripts written by the ancients and by Rabbenu Gershom himself, a rare privilege. According to one legend, Rashi had the good fortune and pleasure of holding in his hands the *Sefer Torah*, the holy scrolls, that his Teacher used during the service.

A number of legal decisions are attributed, rightly or wrongly, to Rabbenu Gershom. Two are famous: on bigamy and on the repudiation of a wife against her will. A third forbids opening another person's mail.

When Rashi arrived in his yeshiva, Rabbenu Gershom was no longer alive. Rashi studied with his successors Rabbi Yaakov ben Yakar, whom he admired and loved more than anyone in the world, David ha-Levi, and Yitzhak ben Yehuda. He was closest to the first, whom he loved for his great modesty and who first made him aware of some rare manuscripts of the Talmud and their Midrashic and other commentators without which it is impossible to study the Talmud in depth. "I owe him everything I know," he wrote, "my understanding, my comprehension, and my heart." Occasionally he accompanied him on his trips to nearby communities and beyond.

After Mainz he went to Worms where there was a large, thriving yeshiva supervised by Rabbi Yitzhak ha-Levi. He stayed there for several years. The reason is clear: at the time, the most renowned centers of higher Jewish learning were in the German Rhineland, though there were also a few in Italy. France became a center only after Rashi's return. By then he was not even thirty years old. He married—but whom? We don't know. We don't even know his wife's name. The couple had three daughters: Miriam, Yokheved, and Rachel. We're equally unsure as to whether they had a fourth daughter; several sources hint that they did, adding that she may have died in infancy.

Did his wife and daughters help Rashi in his vineyards? No

doubt they did . . . *if* he was a wine grower, which has never been fully confirmed. Did he have other sources of income? Nothing is less certain. One legend claims he lived from trade with the Gentiles. There is a letter of Rashi's, written in Germany, revealing that he didn't have the means to support his family: he couldn't afford to buy bread and clothes.

As for the daughters, they are believed to have been erudite. It seems that, sometimes, they were consulted regarding customs and practices in matters of food and family life.

Miriam's husband, Rabbi Yehuda ben Nathan, was a great scholar. And so was Yokheved's husband, Rabbi Meir ben Shmuel. Rachel must have been known for her beauty, for she was nicknamed "*Belle-assez*," "rather beautiful." Her husband, a certain Eliezer, divorced her. Why? We don't know. If she remarried, we don't know whom she married.

On the other hand, we know that Rashi, though married and perhaps already a father, returned to Worms and stayed there several years. Was it because he wasn't ready to found his own yeshiva? As soon as he returned to Troyes, he did found one. His predecessors are known for their learning: Rabbi Eliyahu ben Menahem the Elder of Mans and Rabbi Yosef bar Shmuel Tov-elem of Limoges.

Why does he hardly mention his wife and daughters? Who ran the household? Who kept house for him? Who accompanied him on trips? Could it be that, like other Talmud Sages, his disciples meant more to him than his close family members?

Rashi's influence can be explained by his knowledge of a range of disciplines—the Bible and the Talmud, mathematics and wine growing, astronomy and zoology.

How did he earn his living? Solely from the produce of his vineyard—there again, if he had one? He did write a lot about wines. He had no salary (in those days, rabbis were not paid), and his students received free instruction. In addition, some of his students, who were more or less destitute, requested financial assistance from him for their everyday needs. His foreign students lived in his house. And ate at his table. When one of them married, Rashi organized the wedding in his house.

Here again, we have no idea how he managed to feed so many people, but apparently he did. More precisely: there is no evidence in any source of anyone complaining.

His students, all of them thirsting for knowledge, flocked to him from everywhere, from the provinces and beyond. There were some students who came from Germany and Eastern Europe.

Among his disciples, we find some of the greatest scholars, including his two sons-in-law who became illustrious French Tosafists, as the commentators of the generations after Rashi were known, from the word for "additional." Indeed, he brought them in as collaborators in his work, as consultants, copyists, or proofreaders of manuscripts. Rabbi Yehuda excelled in his way of commenting on the Talmud following Rashi's original approach. After his father-in-law's death, it is he who completed Rashi's commentary of Tractate Makkot (punishments) of the Talmud. Yehuda's son, Rabbi Shmuel (the Rashbam), became a Sage in turn. But the most famous and admired of Rashi's grandsons was Rabbi Meir's son, Yaakov (Jacob), better known as Rabbenu Tam. The same adjective is attributed to the patriarch Jacob in the Scriptures. *Tam* means "complete piety." When he was born, Rashi was nearly sixty.

Rabbenu Tam had a dramatic and even tragic life, enduring periods of danger and suffering. At forty-seven, he was assaulted by hate-filled Crusaders and sustained five head wounds. "You are Israel's greatest," the aggressors yelled. "So we will take revenge on you for our crucified Lord. We will wound you the way you wounded our Lord!" He was already old when the Jewish community in Blois was accused of ritual murder; the rabbi ordered all the Jews of France to observe a day of fasting in solidarity for their endangered brothers and sisters; thirty-one of them lost their lives.

In general, Rashi's disciples, and they were numerous and prolific, identified themselves by the teaching "received from his mouth." If, with time, a true Teacher is defined by the quality of his disciples, Rashi is among the greatest.

Let us recall some of them: Rabbi Shmaya worked at putting his Teacher's notes in order. From him we know that a Christian owed Rashi money and maintained that he had already reimbursed him. Rashi demanded that he make this statement under oath in church. Rabbi Yosef Kara, the author of important books on the Prophets. Rabbi Simhah ben Shmuel of Vitry, who was especially interested in the litanies and prayers written by Rashi. It is thought, without being confirmed, that several of these reflect Rashi's grief and pain at the atrocities committed by the Crusaders. As for his two sons-in-law, cited above, they always refer to his interpretations.

How old was he when he took up his duties as Troyes' official rabbi? By then he was already a respected member of the rabbinical court. No precise date was found in the historical records. The only thing we are certain of is that he was already well known and that his reputation had extended beyond this little city. Before his arrival, the notables went to see outside authorities to settle their differences. Once he became their rabbi, this custom ended. All the problems were brought to him. Questions were sent to him from far-away countries. And his decisions, made with humility but firmly, were never disputed. At the end of his life, often sick and bedridden, he dictated his answers to his correspondents. And he explained the reasons for his decisions.

In his superb book on Rashi, Avraham Grossman, one of his best biographers and a fine essayist, puts forward a captivating idea: Rashi's success and popularity, in all the strata of the Jewish population for a thousand years, cannot be explained by his commentaries alone but are due to his personality as well.

He lists five character traits that have to be taken into account if we are to grasp the reason why his immense work had so much impact: humility and simplicity, the pursuit of the truth, respect for his fellow man, confidence in his own creative inspiration, and the feeling of accomplishing the mission of a community leader.

Was his humility unconscious? Opinion is divided. On the one hand, can authentic modesty not be authentic? On the other, if exaggerated, wouldn't modesty get in the way of courageous research, deny the mind the right to take on an adventure whose goal is to break through the wall and create an opening to renewal?

In studying him tirelessly, we find no trace of arrogance or conceit in Rashi. Exaggerated susceptibility of any kind seems alien to him. Self-confidence, yes, so long as it is not boundless. He sometimes admits to making a mistake on a specific issue. Sometimes—and we'll return to this below— he simply confesses to ignorance. No other Sage did this as frankly and as frequently. The expression is "eini yoden."

Hence his courteous and respectful attitude in his relationships with others. With his enemies and opponents—for he did have some—he betrays no impatience, no irritation. He also becomes a kind of ideal address for his peers and disciples: their queries and problems come to him by the hundreds, from Italy, Germany, and France; they concern trade, marriage and the ritual. His answers form part of his work. Why does he forbid the sick from reciting daily prayers? Is it because, being ill, they are unable to concentrate on the very soul of prayer? Or is it so the sick won't feel guilty that they aren't well enough to recite the required prayer? He showed such an affectionate understanding for others that all assumptions are permitted.

But what about the Christians? What was Rashi's attitude toward them? We will come to that later. For the moment, let us just mention that he viewed their business relationships with the Jews in a favorable light. Did he consider them inevitable? He also made a point of saying that, after all, they were not pagans.

One day he noticed that a Christian with whom he had business dealings didn't really care about his own Christian faith; he was too casual about it. Rashi refused to see him again.

Having said this, it is surprising to note that Rashi didn't take part in the virulent polemics with the Christians on what separates our religious traditions. He could not have been unaware of them. Word of these polemics reached the most remote corners of his region and far beyond. And Rashi, for one, surely understood their possible effects on the community: they often ended badly. Hence his hostility toward Christendom. For him, it symbolized Esau. What he thought of the Christians is what he says about Esau. He shows some understanding, though not completely whole-hearted, for Isaac's brother Ishmael, but none for Jacob's brother. He goes very far in his choice of words in describing the latter's secret thoughts and evil intentions. But of the two brothers, wasn't Jacob the one who, with the help of his mother, Rebecca, deceived his blind father in order to receive the blessings intended for the eldest? No, says Rashi. The lies came from Esau who, being a hypocrite, did everything to please his father so he could be the first blessed.

Another example: the biblical text tells us that on that day Esau returned from the fields tired and famished. Why tired? We could suppose that he had just done some strenuous work. For Rashi the reason is completely different: he was tired of killing. Worse still: Rashi is convinced that Esau was guilty of the three worst transgressions: idolatry, adultery, and murder. In general, he uses Esau—or Edom—as a symbol of everything evil and wicked surrounding Israel.

Often, indeed very often, this animosity is not in the text itself, but in many Midrashic commentaries Rashi cites. But Rashi sets about making a personal choice to support his hypothesis. Since Israel has and will have an enemy, this enemy must be named; it is Christianity, which, in Esau, existed well before the common era.

Grossman stresses this point. According to him, Esau is not the only person Rashi presents in a negative light. He sees other protagonists as having negative traits as well: for him, Lot, Abraham's nephew, did nothing commendable. If he lived in the sinful city of Sodom, it was because he felt comfortable among the impious.

Ishmael? Not attractive either. He kept company with brigands and imitated their habits. Idolatrous and violent, he was not really loved by his father.

How are we to explain these seemingly unjust allegories if not by the more or less hostile political, social, and religious environment of the period? Weren't the people of Israel assailed, threatened, attacked, and tormented by both Christians and Muslims?

A general rule: whenever he can, Rashi chooses passages in the Midrash that can be interpreted as arguments against "the other nations." Why? There again, let us draw on Grossman who attributes Rashi's animosity to theological pressures to which were added the horrendous persecutions Christendom inflicted on the Jews in that part of Europe.

The forced "disputations" in the royal courts and cathedrals, the violent anti-Semitic propaganda that resulted from these, the preparations for the first Crusade whose victims included Rashi's disciples and friends, surely influenced his conception of the world. Was it his reaction to those events that were to leave traces of fire and blood in the Jewish memory forever after?

Did he ever forgive Esau whose descendents—in Rome, according to him—bore down on the Jews whose tragic destiny was supposed to be proof that God had changed his chosen people?

One should read Rashi's commentary on the Song of Songs, a cry of distress and a song of love. It reflects the suffering of the Jews in exile. And so do some of the Psalms. For Rashi, King David predicts the martyrdom of the Righteous who sacrificed themselves in order to sanctify the Name of God.

But let us return to the Scriptures:

Rashi, as opposed to other great interpreters and sages, seems to favor the patriarchs exclusively: although the Talmud never hesitates to describe them as deeply human and mentions their failings and errors, Rashi depicts them as Righteous Men if not absolute saints. No misdemeanor, no blunder, never an ethical shortcoming when it comes to Abraham, Isaac, and Jacob. God is proud of them for all eternity and so is he.

And yet.

Throughout his work, usually what counts most for Rashi is the concern for truth. Revealing the deep, hidden meaning of a biblical verse or a Talmudic statement, the very meaning that our distant precursors had bequeathed to their descendants—that's the ultimate objective of his approach.

An approach that calls for a great deal of daring. Breaking down closed doors, disputing standard interpretations, going beyond the superficial, beyond what meets the eye, reaching higher and higher and delving deep down: courage is needed to aspire to this and consent to it. Rashi has courage, and he shares it with his pupils. In some instances he almost goes too far. Concerning the person of Flavius Josephus, for example.

Flavius Josephus is too demanding of the Jews besieged in Jerusalem. He asks them to resign themselves and accept defeat. He finishes his life as a patrician, near Rome. It is hardly surprising that the Jewish tradition kept its distance from the work of Flavius Josephus, Jewish historian. For centuries, the writer was treated as a marginal figure in the religious literature of the Jewish people. Too moderate, too conciliatory, too weak with regard to the besieging Romans: he was regarded with genuine antipathy. But apparently not by Rashi, who admires his work *The War of the Jews* for having served as the basis for the history book *Yosiphon* by Yosef ben Gurion ha-Cohen.

Rashi's commentaries on the ancient texts are numerous, varied, infinitely original, and sometimes personal; they are found in various contemporaneous and later manuscripts; they include the Torah, the Prophets, the Writings (Proverbs, Song of Songs, Ecclesiastes, Psalms, book of Job—except for the very last chapters, which he did not finish), and, naturally, almost all of the Talmud. One of the most ancient manuscripts, if not the most ancient, is of the Pentateuch, the first of its kind, written by Makir, a renowned thirteenth-century scribe who scrupulously copied the texts written by Rashi himself and corrected by Rabbi Shmaya. Rashi often relies on his precursors; for the Torah, the Aramaic translation by the convert Onkelos, for the Prophets, that of Yonatan ben Uziel; but above all he relies on the Midrash texts, not in order to contradict them, but in order to deepen them by adding his own knowledge. Nevertheless, in some rare instances he makes a point of disagreeing with his own Teachers. But even then he does so with a student's respect for those whose teaching is a legacy. Just to illustrate Rashi's fondness for simplicity, remember the tragedy that befell Aaron's sons Nadav and Avihu who lost their lives because they introduced "an alien fire," says Rashi. "They were drunk."

Let us note that Rashi's commentary on the Bible was the first Hebrew book to be printed: around 1470. It is hardly surprising that it rapidly crossed frontiers and the seas and made its way to the furthermost reaches of Jewish community life in the Diaspora. No other work was so widely circulated. The same is true of his writings on the Babylonian Talmud. Maimonides' commentaries on the Talmud were criticized, often unjustly and sometimes too harshly, but Rashi's were not. His acceptance by nearly all the Jewish thinkers and their disciples remains just about unique. Christian scholars benefited from his commentaries each in his own way—among them the illustrious Nicholas of Lyra, in the thirteenth century, who translated his work into

Latin. He cited Rashi so frequently that a certain Jean Mercier, at the Collège Royal of Paris, nicknamed him Simius Solomnis, Solomon's (Shlomo's) ape.

Through Nicholas of Lyra, Rashi had a powerful influence on Martin Luther, whose German translation of the Bible owes much to him.

In subsequent pages, we will speak about his inexhaustible curiosity, his inventive genius, his touching humility in the presence of texts and their interpreters: he, the most illustrious of scholars, who mastered both sacred texts and secular ones (he had a knowledge of the sciences, and of French, Greek, and Arabic), was never embarrassed to admit that he couldn't grasp the true meaning of a text, that a literal or hermeneutic translation escaped him or just seemed obscure. And in that case, it had to be elucidated at all costs. What is unclear initially will become clear the second time around. What is hidden will be revealed. For him, everything must remain open, comprehensible. A decision maker, he adapts the Law to present needs.

According to some, he was also a mystic (a staunch believer in miracles—and not just the biblical ones of the past—he believed that at the advent of the Messianic era, the Third Temple would descend from heaven). But he was in many ways a scientific rationalist, making accessible and familiar things that are not. Nothing is meant to remain complicated forever. The Torah is not up in the heavens, unchanging, among the angels and seraphs, but here down below. It is up to men to interpret it and reinterpret it anew each day.

A linguist and grammarian, if he finds the Aramaic or Hebrew insufficient, Rashi resorts to German and particularly to French or "Belaaz" in gloss, or the tongue of the Gentiles; and Rashi uses the latter abundantly: we find more than a thousand French words in his works. Scholars still study him today for the light he sheds on the French language in the early Middle Ages: some terms aren't found anywhere else.

In general, intent on finding the right word and the suitable literary style to explain a biblical or Talmudic expression or law, when he is free to choose among different approaches, he opts for the simplest, most reasonable, most accessible one.

In delving into Rashi's commentaries on the Babylonian Talmud one sometimes comes across contradictions. Tosafists and researchers have stated it unambiguously: there is no doubt that Rashi changed his mind on some particular points. For what reason? Was this due to the erroneous judgments of copyists, or Rashi's own intellectual honesty? After all, over the years, going from one discovery to next, one can admit to having made a mistake. Ultimately, as in all real spiritual and scholarly quests, all assumptions of sudden reversals are permissible.

Let us listen to his grandson, the Rashbam:

"Rabbi Shlomo, my grandfather, the Light of the Exile, who interpreted the Torah, the Prophets, and the Writings, made every effort to elucidate the natural meaning of the text, and I, Shmuel ben Meir, often discussed his commentaries with him or in his presence. And he admitted to me that, if he had the time, he would revise his work taking into account explanations that are revealed day after day."

Let us repeat it:

In his writings, he never hesitates to admit that he doesn't know the answer to a question, or the solution to a difficulty. For example: in the book of Genesis (28:5), the text says Isaac sent Jacob "to Padan-aram unto Laban, son of Bethuel the Syrian, the brother of Rebecca, Jacob's and Esau's mother." The sentence is long and unwieldy, and full of superfluous details: at this point in the narrative is there anyone who doesn't know who Rebecca is? Rashi's commentary: "I admit that I don't know what this verse wants to tell us." The author of *Siftei Hakhamim* responded with blunt words: "There are some among us who are surprised that Rashi feels compelled to tell us he doesn't know; if he doesn't know, let him be silent." But Rashi believes in being frank and truthful. If he doesn't know, he feels he should tell us.

Is it due to the breadth of his knowledge? To the luminous quality of his style, clear and captivating, always tight, precise, sober, attracting the reader's allegiance? His desire to have a dialogue with students? Sometimes students have tant is the lesson that is learned from it: the need for modesty on the part of the great; they should always consult with humbler men.

For another glimpse of how Rashi sees God's role in the creation of man, we look to the next chapter, in which the creation is told in a different narrative. "And the Lord God said, It is not good that the man should be alone" (Genesis 2:18).

Rashi['s question: Why is it bad for there to be only one human being? His answer]: So that it won't be said that two powers reign in the world. Up high, one with no female companion, and below, one with no female companion.

"I will make him a fitting helper for him" (literally, a "helper facing" or "opposed to him").

Rashi's question: How is she both a help and in opposition? Rashi's answer: If he is deserving, the other will help him; if he is not, the other will fight against him.

Playing on the words *ish*—"man"—and *ishah*—"woman"—which is valid only in Hebrew, Rashi demonstrates that the holy tongue was used at the time of the creation of the world.

"And the Lord God caused a deep sleep to fall upon Adam, and he slept."

Here Rashi puts forward a touching explanation for why he put Adam to sleep: God is about to operate on Adam's ribs and make his future companion out of one of them; if Adam suspects this, it might disgust him forever.

A surprising idea:

And (seeing woman for the first time) "Adam said, this is now bone of my bones, and flesh of my flesh."

This means that Adam had already mated with beasts and animals, but was satisfied only when uniting with his spouse. Another odd comment in the story of the Garden of Eden:

"Now the serpent was more subtle than any beast of the field . . . and he said unto the woman . . ." What is the serpent doing in the Garden of Eden? And what aroused his interest? He saw man and woman united sexually, says the commentator, and this excited him.

The serpent persuaded Eve to taste the forbidden fruit in spite of the danger that she could die. Then she gave it to Adam so he would share it with her.

Rashi: she was afraid that she would die and that Adam would survive her and marry another woman.

Once God has confronted them about the eating of the fruit, the man defends himself with the following verse:

"And the man said, The woman whom thou gavest to be with me, she gave me of the tree, and I did eat."

Rashi: here Adam shows his lack of gratitude to God for giving him the woman.

The serpent, too, is dealt with.

"And the Lord God said unto the serpent . . . upon thy belly shalt thou go."

Rashi, true to his undeviating attachment to the literal text, deduces from this that originally the serpent had legs but then he lost them.

"So he drove out the man; and he placed . . . a flaming sword (*lame* in Belaaz), which turned every way" at the entrance of the Garden of Eden.

There is a Midrash on this verse, says Rashi, but my aim is to remain with the straightforward meaning.

Life outside the Garden also offers much for Rashi to explore. God accepts Abel's offering but not Cain's. And the latter kills. "And the Lord said unto Cain, Where is Abel thy brother? And he said . . . am I my brother's keeper?" God reprimands him: "What hast thou done? the voice of thy brother's blood (in plural) cryeth unto me from the ground." Rashi explains the plural: "The blood of thy brother, and also of his descendants."

In other words: he who kills, kills more than the victim.

. . .

Ten generations after the creation, in the time of Noah, "And God saw that the wickedness of man was great. . . . And it repented the Lord that he had made man on the earth, and it grieved him at his heart."

Rashi's commentary: "It grieved him to have lost what he had created. Just like the king who became sad because of his son. And this is how I answered the question a heathen asked Rabbi Yehoshua ben Korkha: "Don't you believe that God can foresee the future?" "Yes," the Sage replied. "But," said the heathen, "it is written that it grieved him at his heart!" "Have you ever had a son?" the Sage asked him. "Yes," said the heathen. "And what did you do when he was born?" "I rejoiced, and I was eager for others to rejoice." "But didn't you know that he would die one day?" "All in good time."

"These are the generations of Noah: Noah was a just man and perfect in his generations." Rashi asks, why the qualifying phrase "in his generations"? He answers: some of our Teachers interpret this as praise: if he had lived in a generation of Righteous Men, he would have been much more righteous. But some teachers see a criticism contained in that verse: by the standard of his generation (of sinners) he was righteous, but in Abraham's generation, he wouldn't have been seen as worth anything.

. . .

"The earth also was corrupt before God, and the country was filled with violence."

Rashi: the reference is to sexuality and violent theft. Wherever we encounter prostitution, it announces the end. Confusion dominates the world and kills both the good and the wicked.

Another ten generations pass, and we pick up our story with Abraham and Sarah.

"Now Sarai Abram's wife bore him no children: and she had an handmaid, an Egyptian, whose name was Hagar" (Genesis 16:1).

Rashi: she was a daughter of the Pharaoh. Having seen the miracles accomplished for Sarah, the Pharaoh said: better that my daughter be a servant in that man's house than a mistress in another man's house.

And Sarai, after waiting ten years, gave Hagar as a concubine to her husband, Abram. "And he went in unto Hagar, and she conceived."

Rashi: on the very first night. But . . . she will have a miscarriage. And conceive again.

Hagar became arrogant. Sarai, offended, angry at her husband, said to him, "The Lord judge between me and thee."

Her position, according to Rashi, is the following: When you prayed to God for a child, you thought only of yourself; it was you who wanted a child. You should have prayed for both of us. And then you see my humiliation and you say nothing!

The story of Abraham and Sarah's desire for children is interrupted by the story of Sodom, the sinful city par excellence, which fell so low in its decline that God decided to "go down . . . and see."

Rashi: as with the story of the Tower of Babel, how is it conceivable that God above doesn't see what is happening below? This verse is here to teach us the law: that in cases involving capital punishment, it is the judges' responsibility not to judge from afar: they should look into everything before reaching a verdict. And here, despite Abraham's defense of the city, the verdict is that it will be destroyed.

Eventually Abraham and Sarah's prayers are answered, and Sarah fulfills a prophecy by giving birth to a son, Isaac, named for his mother's laughter at the thought that they would have a child in their advanced age. When Isaac was weaned, Abraham made a great feast and all the notables attended. Suddenly Sarah saw Hagar's son *metzakhek*, laughing.

As we said above, Rashi is harsh with him. He translates the word *metzakhek* differently, to suggest that Ishmael committed the sins of idolatry, sexual acts, and murder. He is not as harsh as he will be with Esau, but enough to make us frown.

And this, in the same spirit:

And Sarah said to Abraham: "Cast out this bondwoman and her son: for the son of this bondwoman shall not be heir with my son, even with Isaac."

Rashi: from Sarah's answer it is clear that the two boys quarreled over the inheritance. Ishmael claimed this right, being the eldest. Sometimes they also went out into the fields where Ishmael shot arrows at Isaac.

This isn't in the text? There must be a Midrash hinting at it, and we can trust Rashi: he'll find it.

Rashi is fond of Sarah, the matriarch. When God tells Abraham to "hearken unto her voice," in other words, to obey her, Rashi attributes prophetic virtues to her.

As for Abraham, he grants Sarah's request, and sends Ishmael away in the wilderness with his mother. Abraham gives them bread and water. But no money, says Rashi. Because of whom? Because of the son who probably took the wrong path in life. As for Hagar, in leaving Abraham and Sarah's house, she returned to her native customs.

However, in the end, God will take pity on them. An angel called to Hagar, "God hath heard the voice (and sobs) of the lad where he is." And Hagar saw a well of water in front of her.

Rashi: the point is he is judged according to his present

deeds. For the angels in heaven refuse to have pity on Ishmael, saying: God of the universe, how can you save someone from dying of thirst when in the future his descendants will kill Abraham's descendants by making them die of thirst? And God replies: man is not judged for his future deeds but for his present ones.

"And it came to pass after these things, that God did tempt Abraham."

In this passage, one of the most moving and meaningful in the Scriptures, Rashi feels he must dwell on many verses and words. In his opening remarks, he wonders after "what things"? The answer—or rather answers—are in the Midrash. Some of our Teachers, he explains, say this: after Satan's words accusing Abraham of ingratitude. Never in any of the feasts that Abraham held in honor of his son did he consider sacrificing a single bull or ram to You. God answered Satan: everything he did, he did for his son; yet if I were to ask him to sacrifice that son, he would.

And another version: "After the words the two brothers exchanged. Ishmael said with pride: (I am worthier than you) for I was thirteen when I was circumcised. Isaac answered him: Are you trying to impress me with just one organ of your body? If God asks me, 'Sacrifice your entire self,' I would do it."

Strange, there was a High Priest named Ishmael, and a sage too. And there was no Rabbi Esau among our great teachers or servants of the Lord.

And God said (to Abraham): "Take now thy son."

Rashi corrects the meaning of this verse to stress the complicity between God and his faithful ally and messenger: God *requests* that Abraham submit to this last trial so that people will not say that the previous ones had no value.

It's worth noting the method that Rashi employs, which the rabbis of the Talmud also used; he takes a biblical statement by God but breaks it up with other statements, not actually found in the Bible, that subtly shift or elucidate the meaning of God's words, as if God were in fact responding to challenges or questions from Abraham. In the Bible, the verse has God saying simply: "Take they son, thy only son, whom thou lovest, Isaac." Rashi breaks the request apart:

Take now thy son.

Rashi: Abraham replied: I have two sons. "Thine only son," said God. "Each one is the only son for his mother," said Abraham. "The one whom thou lovest," said God. "I love both of them," said Abraham. "Isaac," said God. Rashi is surprised by the length of this dialogue: why didn't God tell him everything right away? So as not to upset him and cause him to lose his mind. And also so he would love the commandment; and could be rewarded for every word spoken. And this is why the father and son spend three days on the road. So people won't say that Abraham acted in a fit of insanity.

Let us appreciate Rashi's boldness: in this moment of sublime tragedy, the deeply human Abraham could have become insane.

"And Abraham took the wood . . . and laid it upon Isaac his son. And he took the fire in his hand and a knife; and they went both of them together."

Putting all the weight of the unquestionably traumatic experience on Abraham, Rashi says: "Abraham, who knew he was going to slay his son, walked with the same willingness and joy as Isaac who knew nothing."

In the Midrashic literature there are a great many legends dealing with this walk and giving the son his own role to play. It is odd that Rashi is so sparing in his commentaries here.

But he will be less so in the following passage.

"And the angel of the Lord called unto him out of heaven, and said [Rashi: with tenderness], Abraham, Abraham: and he said, Here I am. And he [the angel] said, 'Lay not thine hand upon the lad, neither do thou any thing unto him: for now I know that thou fearest God.' "

The text is clear, precise, concise. Outwardly Abraham accepts everything in silence. But Rashi is not satisfied. He who usually likes simplicity and brevity at all times suddenly brings up a dialogue from the Midrash, cited by Rabbi Abba, between Abraham and God: "Abraham says: I would like to talk to you. Yesterday you told me that Isaac would be my descendant; then you told me to take my son (sacrifice him to you) and now you tell me not to lay a hand upon the lad!" In other words: how can God say one thing and its opposite? And behold God answers him and his answer is simply astounding. "I don't change my commands"; it is you who have misunderstood me! I asked you to (take your son) and climb up (the mountain) with him. I didn't ask you to slay him!"

What! The whole episode concerning Isaac's near sacrifice would be based on a mere misunderstanding!

There are other legends, other exchanges in the Midrash, depicting Abraham as tenacious and determined to obtain from God more promises, both old and new, for his descendants. But Rashi, for unexplained reasons, hardly touches on these.

"And Sarah died."

Rashi feels the need to comment on how close the *Akedah* (the sacrifice of Isaac) is to the death of his mother: it is when she learned of the event that her soul left her.

Here again, the Midrash elaborates on this at greater

length, stressing the part played by Satan. Why doesn't Rashi use it? Could it be that this episode troubles him more deeply than others?

Isaac of course survives his ordeal and his father sends an emissary to bring back a bride for him from the land of Abraham's family:

> Then Laban and Bethuel answered (to Eliezer, Abraham's envoy).

Laban has a bad reputation with Rashi:

"Laban was ungodly: he had the arrogance to speak before his father." The same applies to Bethuel: a negative individual. When Rebecca's brother and mother answer and give their consent, letting her go to marry Isaac, Rashi asks: but where was Bethuel? And he replies: an angel killed him because he tried to prevent the marriage.

A historical precedent for the supporters of women's rights: before Rebecca's departure, her brother and mother ask her whether she agrees. She replies with just one word, "*Eilekh*": "I will go." Rashi: the meaning here is I will go even if you are opposed to it.

Rashi: we can deduce from this that we have no right to force a woman to marry someone; we need her consent.

An odd story of malicious gossip: even the first patriarch wasn't spared. The text first:

And these are the generations of Isaac, Abraham's son: Abraham begat Isaac.

Rashi wonders: why this repetition? His answer: having mentioned Isaac, Abraham's son, the following statement was necessary. For there were gossipers who said that since Sarah was childless during the years when she lived with Abraham, Isaac's father was really King Elimelekh and not Abraham. What did God do? He gave Isaac the same facial features as Abraham. So when they saw the striking resemblance, everyone could see that Isaac was Abraham's son.

Isaac and Rebecca go on to have their own sons, twins Jacob and Esau who are at odds even before they leave the womb. In discussing Rashi's suspicious attitude toward Ishmael, we also mentioned his contempt for Esau. Let us point out another instance:

At a certain point in the narrative about Isaac and Rebecca, the text says that Esau was forty years old when he married Judith, the daughter of Beeri the Hittite and Basemath the daughter of Elon the Hittite. Rashi seizes the opportunity to add this: Esau looked like a boar. When a boar lies down, he stretches out his legs as if to show how pure he is. . . . For forty years, Esau stole women from their husbands and tortured them. So his father said to him: I married when I was forty, do the same.

In Isaac's old age, he prepares to bless his firstborn, favorite son, Esau. But Rebecca has other plans, and sends Jacob in Esau's stead. Did Jacob lie to his blind father by impersonating Esau? No, says Rashi, always prepared to defend Jacob against his brother. When Jacob says to his father, "I am Esau, thy firstborn," Rashi changes the punctuation and the meaning of the words: "I am who I am (the one who brings you your favorite food), and Esau is thy firstborn." And when Isaac asks him, "Are you my son Esau?" he doesn't answer, "I am he," but "It is I." There again, for Rashi, Jacob doesn't lie and never will.

Rashi goes very far: when Isaac, "trembling very exceedingly," says to Esau, "thy brother came '*be-mirmah*' and hath taken away thy blessing," he translates the word *be-mirmah*, meaning "with cunning," as *be-hokhmah*, meaning "with wisdom and intelligence."

Rebecca was told that Esau was "proposing to kill Jacob." Told by whom? Whom could Esau have possibly confided in? In his mother? Surely not. In his father? Surely not again. Rashi has a ready answer: "it is the Holy Spirit that told her everything." Even He is against Esau.

. . .

Jacob's entire life is a series of miracles. Even a small, ordinary detail partakes of the supernatural.

Jacob left Beersheba and went toward Haran. (At a certain place), he saw "the sun was set; and took of the stones of that place, and put them for his pillows." Rashi: one stone said, the Righteous Man will rest his head on me, and the other said, no, on me. So God fused them and made them into one, which He placed under Jacob's head. And that's when he fell asleep. And in a dream he saw the ladder with its top touching heaven. But where was the ladder placed? On Mount Moriah where the Temple will later be built. But . . . geographically isn't this impossible? The spot where Jacob was lying was far away? Easy: on that night, Mount Moriah was uprooted and transported to the spot where Jacob was resting.

One more miracle.

Let us return to the wicked Laban. When he meets Jacob, his future son-in-law, he embraces him. What could be more natural? No, says Rashi: "He embraces him so he could go through his pockets, which he thought were full of gold coins." Laban embraces him also "to see if he has precious pearls in his mouth," says Rashi.

"And Jacob loved Rachel; and said (to Laban), I will serve thee seven years for Rachel thy younger daughter."

Rashi's commentary:

Why so many details? Because Jacob felt that Laban was an inveterate liar. He said to him: I will serve for Rachel, but if you think you can tell me that we're referring to another Rachel, off the street," let me be specific: "thy daughter." And in case you say you'll change her name to Leah and Leah's to Rachel, let me say to you right away: "your younger daughter, the youngest." But, adds Rashi, in spite of all these precautions, Laban betrayed him.

On the night of the wedding, Laban brought Leah to Jacob, who became aware of Laban's betrayal when he woke up.

Rashi: actually, all night long Jacob was convinced his bride was Rachel. As a precaution, he had given her a secret sign of recognition. But when Rachel realized what was happening, she revealed the secret to her older sister so she wouldn't be put to shame.

Marvelous Rachel, Rashi says: when, with the years, she became jealous of her sister, she envied her for her good deeds.

Jacob continues to serve Laban, and marries Rachel as well. He becomes rich, and leaves Laban's household, returning to the land where his angry brother Esau abides.

And Jacob sent messengers to his brother whose arrival he feared. He said to them: "Thus shall ye speak unto my lord Esau; Thy servant Jacob saith thus, I have sojourned with Laban."

Rashi: I didn't become a lord or an important dignitary but a stranger. You have no reason to hate me: the blessings I received from our father did not come to pass. And also this: I lived in Laban's house and learned nothing from his evil deeds.

Praise for Jacob:

Having learned that Esau was coming to meet him with four hundred men, Jacob was greatly afraid.

Rashi: faced with this imminent conflict, Jacob felt a double fear: the fear of being killed and/or of killing others.

Jacob's prayer: "Deliver me . . . from the hand of my brother, from the hand of Esau." Rashi's commentary: deliver me from my brother who doesn't behave like a brother but like Esau, the ungodly one.

Another miracle: Jacob, on his journey, wrestles with an angel. After their morning duel, the angel asks Jacob what his name is, and Jacob tells him. "Thy name shall be called no more Jacob," says the angel, "but Israel: for as a prince hast thou power with God and with men, and hast prevailed."

Rashi dwells on just two words: "No more Jacob (You are no longer Jacob) for you didn't obtain blessings through cheating but openly and with dignity."

The two enemy brothers finally meet. "And Esau ran to meet him (Jacob) and embraced him . . . and they wept."

In the biblical text, there are two small dots on the word *embraced.*

In his commentary, Rashi, suddenly charitable toward Esau, says that faced with Jacob's humility, Esau could not help feeling compassionate. Still, he cites another source according to which he would not have been wholeheartedly compassionate.

Jacob introduces his family to his brother. First the hand-maids, then Leah with her children, then Joseph and Rachel. Rashi is surprised: why not Rachel and Joseph? Commentary: Joseph said to himself that his mother was a great beauty; she might attract the attention of the impious one. I had better step in between them.

"So Esau returned that day on his way unto Seir." Rashi wonders why the verb is in the singular. Because he was alone. One after the other, the four hundred men who had been with him, deserted him.

As for Jacob, he comes out of the ordeal, arriving in Shechem "whole." Rashi's commentary: "whole in his healed body, whole in his wealth, and whole in his faith."

Odd: here Rashi does not mention his family.

Dina, Jacob's only daughter, is raped by Prince Hamor's son Shechem. Hamor tries to make up for the misdeed and proposes to the victim's brothers and their father Jacob that the two youths marry. After a long discussion, Dina's brothers suggest *be-mirmah*, with cunning (like Jacob with Isaac), that they could come to an arrangement providing all the men in the tribe get circumcised.

Once again, as in the first instance, Rashi translates the word as "wisdom or intelligence."

On the third day after the operation, when the men opposite were most sore, Jacob's sons, Simeon and Levi, attack the city and kill all the males.

Like Jacob later, Rashi does not justify their act of revenge. He says: why does the text mention that they were Jacob's sons? Because they were. But they behaved as though they were not: they did not seek his advice.

"And Jacob dwelt . . . in the land of Canaan. These are the generations of Jacob. Joseph, being seventeen years old . . ." The proximity if not the continuity of these two verses arouses Rashi's interest. Several commentaries. Let us cite two:

A. The aim of the text is to emphasize the great resemblance between Jacob and Joseph. First of all, physically. But also in another way: they had the same destiny. One was hated, the other too. One had a brother who tried to kill him, the other too.

B. The text also aims to show that, at this stage of his life, Jacob wished to live peacefully and then the story of Joseph befell him. It is as though the Holy One, Blessed be He, had said: really, all these Righteous Men, is it not sufficient for them that they will have their share in the world to come, that they wish to live peacefully in this one too?

As though Rashi, here, wished to explain the suffering of Israel in exile. . . .

"And he is a lad (or adolescent)."

Rashi's commentary: Joseph behaves like an immature adolescent. He dresses his hair, touches up his eyes; he does everything to look handsome.

Rashi's portrait of Joseph is not attractive. Admittedly he keeps company with the servant girls' children, but he has no hesitation about undermining the existence of Leah's children. He tells their father unpleasant things about them: that they eat meat carved out of the flesh of living animals, that they mistreat the servant girls' children, call them slaves, and engage in all kinds of sexual acts.

He will be punished for these three things.

And the brothers, annoyed by Joseph's grandiose dreams, decided to kill him: "and we shall see what will become of his dreams."

Rashi: Rabbi Yitzhak said: the verse must be divided in half. The part dealing with the decision belongs to the brothers; the last part to the Holy Spirit. It is God who says; do what you wish, and we'll see what will become of it.

Rather than kill him, on Judah's advice, the brothers decide to sell Joseph into slavery.

(Rashi: Joseph will be sold several times: first to the Ishmaelites, who sold him to the Midianites, who in turn sold him to the Egyptians.)

The brothers kill a goat and dip Joseph's beautiful coat in its blood. Seeing it, Jacob cries out: "It is my son's coat; an evil beast hath devoured him."

Rashi is surprised: why didn't the Holy Spirit—on whom Jacob usually depended until then—reveal the truth to him? Because the brothers put a ban on anyone who would. Question: Isaac was still alive and he knew; why didn't he put his son's mind at rest? Because he said to himself: if God doesn't reveal the truth to him, by what right can I? Consequence:

they each certainly had their reasons, but the unfortunate Jacob mourned for twenty-two long years.

"And all his sons and all his daughters (in the plural) rose up to comfort him."

Rashi wonders: where do these daughters come from? (Jacob has only one, Dina!) He quotes Rabbi Yehuda: the founding father of each tribe had a twin sister. Rabbi Yehuda says: these daughters were the Canaanite women whom the sons had married—daughters that were really daughters-in-law.

"And it came to pass at that time, that Judah went down from his brethren."

Rashi is surprised: why is the story of the selling of Joseph interrupted to tell a story that is unrelated to it: the affair of Judah and Tamar? The answer: the text teaches us that the brothers resented Judah for the advice he had given them; he really should just have told them to bring their brother back home.

Indeed, the Talmud also has a low opinion of Judah: depriving a man of his freedom is a serious transgression.

. . .

The story of the widow Tamar, Judah's daughter-in-law, is remarkable. As she sits by the wayside and her face is veiled, Judah mistakes her for a whore. He has no money on him, so he gives her his signet and bracelets as a pledge. Then she discovers she is pregnant. A public scandal: Judah's daughter-in-law is guilty of adultery! She is sentenced to be burned. So she sends the signet and bracelets to her father-in-law and says: I am pregnant by their owner.

Rashi's commentary: why didn't she name him? To avoid humiliating him. Indeed, she was prepared to die in the flames rather than humiliate him. Hence the saying of our Sages: it is better to throw oneself into a furnace than shame someone in public.

And because Tamar behaved with so much dignity and modesty, some of her descendants will be kings of Israel.

"And Joseph was well favored . . ." in the home of Potiphar, the chief steward of Pharaoh, in which he was a slave.

Rashi: as he thought of himself as important and in power, he began to indulge in food and drink, and fixed his hair with care. So the Holy One, Blessed be He, said: your father is mourning and you strut about. . . . Fine, I'll send a bear upon you.

The bear of desire, of instinct . . . Potiphar's wife falls in love with him. The opportunity arises on the day when everyone is at the fair except Potiphar's wife and Joseph: she pretends to be unwell. And Joseph has work to do in the house.

Rashi cites a nice discussion between Rav and Shmuel. One says: he really had work. The other says: of course not, he was going to give in to his lust. He was about to . . . but suddenly his father's face appeared before his eyes. This saved him.

Rejected by Joseph, she complained to her husband and accused the Jewish servant of trying to rape her. And her husband believed her? Yes, says Rashi, she told him about it while they were making love.

However, Potiphar does not disappear from the scene.

Several passages later, Joseph's ability to interpret dreams has taken him from prison to the court of Pharaoh, where he is already enjoying quasi-absolute power when a certain Potipherah, priest of On, gives him his daughter Asenath in marriage. Rashi then identifies Potipherah as Potifar and says: he was given this new name because he became a eunuch for having tried, in turn, to seduce Joseph.

And what about his brothers in all this? And Jacob?

They are suffering. All the inhabitants of Canaan are suffering. A dreadful famine is devastating the land. The only place where people have food is in Egypt. Jacob knows what to do. The text says: "Joseph's ten brethren went to buy corn in Egypt."

Rashi's commentary: why "Joseph's brethren" and not "Jacob's sons"? Because they had repented; they regretted having sold him. They are now determined to love him and buy him back for as much money as is asked of them.

They are arrested and brought before Joseph. He recognizes them, but they don't recognize him: the last time they saw him he had no beard. Is it to punish them? He doesn't reveal who he is. He accuses them of being spies. They protest: "we are all one man's sons; we are true men."

Rashi: though the brothers don't know it, it is the Holy Spirit that is speaking through their lips: indeed, they have the same father.

They tell him the truth: we are twelve sons, "the youngest is this day with our father, and one is not."

Rashi cites a Midrash: "And if you find him and are asked a large sum of money in order to free him, would you pay it? Yes, they said. And if you're told that he'll never be returned to you, what would you do? We came to kill or be killed, they said. Ah, didn't I say so? You came to kill the people of this city, said Joseph. In fact, I have divined by my goblet that two of you destroyed the great city of Shechem.

He "took from them Simeon, and bound him before their eyes."

Rashi: why does the text say in front of his brothers? Because once they left, he was freed and given food and drink.

Joseph demands that they fetch their youngest brother, Benjamin. Jacob refuses to let him leave. Reuben insists: "Slay my two sons, if I bring him not to thee."

Rashi: Jacob says, my eldest son is a fool. He tells me to slay his sons, but aren't they also mine?

But the famine is severe, and Judah convinces Jacob to let them return to Egypt for more food. Once there, however, Joseph plays a trick on them and takes from them Benjamin, the other son of Rachel. The brothers beg Joseph to free their younger brother. Joseph finally felt pity for his brother, and he went alone to his chamber and wept.

Rashi pinpoints the moment of pity: Joseph questions Benjamin: do you have a brother by the same mother? I had one, said Benjamin, but I don't know where he is. Do you have children? Yes, says Benjamin. I have sons. What are their names? Joseph asks. All their names are related to the name of my absent brother, says Benjamin. This is when Joseph feels tears coming to his eyes.

It all ends well. A moving reconciliation scene. Joseph sends off his brothers to bring back their father. He warns them: do not quarrel on the road.

For Rashi, thinking like a rabbi, this injunction not to quarrel means "do not discuss *halakhah*, Jewish law"—as if to say that to discuss Jewish law is to argue about it. But then he prefers the simpler interpretation; Joseph is afraid that they'll start blaming one another: it is you who maligned him . . . it was your idea to sell him . . . you who incited us to hate him . . .

"And Jacob lived in the land of Egypt seventeen years."

Rashi: At the end of his life Jacob wished to reveal to his children the end of exile, of all exile, but he could not.

"And Israel beheld Joseph's sons, and said, Who are these?"

Rashi: he tried to bless them, but the *Shekhinah*, God's feminine attribute, left him because Jeroboam and Achav (impious kings) will be born from Ephraim and Jehu and his sons from Menasseh.

Yet nonetheless he will bless them later: judge Gideon will be born from one and Joshua from the other.

In his farewell blessings, once again, Jacob tried to reveal to his children the secret of redemption. And once again the *Shekhinah* departed from him.

So he spoke of something else.

After Jacob's funeral, the brothers say to Joseph: "Thy father did command before he died, saying, So shall ye say unto

Joseph, Forgive . . . the trespass of thy brethren, and their sin." But this is not true. Jacob never said any such thing.

Rashi's commentary: it was for the sake of peace that they didn't tell the truth. Since then, the Talmud imposed this rule: one has the right to lie if it is for the sake of peace.

3

Israel, the People, and the Land

Rashi believes, following all the Midrashic literature, that the people of Israel live and act at the center of the history of men and of nations. A feeling of superiority? No, of singularity.

Why does the city of Hebron hold a special place in the biblical geography? Its name is Kiryat Arba, the city of the four. Four couples have their graves there: Adam and Eve, Abraham and Sarah, Isaac and Rebecca, Jacob and Leah, in other words the fathers and mothers of humanity.

God gave the prophets to Israel alone. This was Moses's wish. He requested it of the Lord. Who granted his wish? Balaam? Balaam, says Rashi, was a visionary, not a prophet. "The *Shekhinah* depends on the prophets only thanks to Israel." Why did the angel take a live coal and burn the lips of the great prophet Isaiah? Because he said too many unkind things about his people.

· · ·

Why the choice of Israel? Is it because of the alliance with Abraham and God's promise to him, to him and his descendants? Is it because of his faithfulness even during his trials? Is it because of the fact that the Lord offered the Torah to all the nations of the earth (including the children of Ishmael and Esau), but they all turned it down, except Israel? Rashi considers all these possibilities and actually includes them all.

God loves his people, says Rashi, citing, as always, Talmudic sources. His biblical commentaries, especially the Song of Songs, are bristling with this conviction, as are his commentaries on the Talmud.

God's true suffering? It comes from seeing Israel and the *Shekhinah* in exile, which is the worst of trials. Though suffering is the consequence of sins committed against Him, He loves Israel in spite of everything. The God of Abraham vowed to never abandon his descendants; he vowed never to substitute Israel for another people, for the people of Israel are never entirely guilty even in their worst sins.

Example:

During the episode of the Golden Calf, the text says: "He (Aaron) received them (the golden earrings) at their hands, and . . . made it a molten calf: and they said: These be thy gods, O Israel, which brought you up out of the land of Egypt." Why "thy gods" and not "our gods"? Rashi quotes the Midrash: we can deduce from this that a mixed multitude had left Egypt and gathered against Aaron. It is these people (and not Israel) who fashioned the golden calf and incited Israel to follow it.

In general, Rashi did everything he could to defend his people.

"God comes from the Sinai": it is like a fiancé who goes to meet his chosen woman.

Israel is wedded to the *Shekhinah*. If anyone goes against Israel, it is as if he were going against the Holy One, Blessed be He.

Grossman stresses this point in his aforementioned book. Contrary to what the first Christians and some of their relatives claimed, the God of Israel did not change people and He never will: the people of Israel remain the *true* Israel for all time.

Naturally, Rashi talks a lot about the land of Israel, which has a special place in the eyes of God: the commandments fulfilled there have a greater significance than if they are fulfilled elsewhere. Rashi goes so far as to insinuate that it is a sin for a Jew to live far from Israel. "The land of Israel cannot tolerate the presence of those who violate the Law of the Torah."

In the passage cited at the beginning of the Tanach, in which he explains why the Bible begins with the creation of the earth and not with the laws, he proclaims unambiguously the right of the people of Israel to the land of Israel. And he repeats this in other works, in various ways and contexts, as when he writes about the hope of redemption and waiting for the Messiah.

Peace

Echoing the Talmud, Rashi, in his commentaries, celebrates the virtues of peace, a Jewish and human ideal that applies to the individual as well as to collective groups, both Jewish and non-Jewish.

What is peace? It is charity and compassion among men. Rashi says this in a Talmudic commentary.

The Flood was the result of the quarrels that dominated the generation of that period, says Rashi. And it shows the greatness of peace. Had the people aspired to peace, they would have been saved.

When the people of Israel are united and in peace, says Rashi, the Name of God is praised on high.

He goes much further in citing a Talmudic legend: great is the value of peace, for even if the people of Israel worship idols, as long as they maintain peace in their ranks, Satan will refrain from intervening.

In one responsum, he says:

Value peace. . . . Peace will be useful to you in saving you from the one who is persecuting you. Satan will no longer reign over you. Our Sages have already asserted it: great is peace, for it was entrusted to the Righteous and not to the impious. May He whose Name and blessing are Peace, gratify us with peace.

Study

In glorifying a thirst for study of the Torah, Rashi comments on the verse "In loving the Lord" as follows: "Don't say, I'll study the Law in order to become rich, to be dignified as Teacher, to receive rewards; rather in all your actions, let yourself be guided only by love of the Torah."

In interpreting the book of Job, Rashi states, "The Torah is maintained thanks to the efforts expended in learning it."

Elsewhere he remarks: "True, it is difficult to abandon the Torah, but it is still better to be attached to it."

"And you will teach your children" refers to your pupils. The Teacher must regard them as his own children, just as, for them, he is their father.

(In the Talmud the law on ransoms is meaningful: if I have the choice of paying a ransom for my father or my teacher, the teacher takes precedence.)

Also: "It is with high spirits, goodwill, and enthusiasm that we must study the Torah."

And this: it is incumbent on a student to respect his Teacher. To avoid embarrassing him, the student should withhold questions that the Teacher might not be able to answer, and then seek a new Teacher.

Compassion

When Rashi recalls Moses's remarkable fate, he often refers to his great compassion for his brothers burdened and oppressed in Egypt.

"He saw them suffer and wept." And further on: "And he (Moses) saw them as they suffered," Rashi adds, "and his heart became heavy." For Rashi, the grandeur of the Teacher-Prophet lies in this ability to suffer with the victims.

True, Moses could not endure the sight of his suffering brothers. Because they were Jewish, and hence his brothers? No, because they were suffering.

The Pharaoh increased pressure on his Jewish slaves: he deprived them of the materials needed to build the pyramids and yet demanded a greater output. "Then the officers of the Children of Israel came and cried unto Pharaoh, saying, Wherefore dealest thou thus with thy servants?"

Rashi's surprising commentary: because the officers

showed such compassion for their brothers, they were later rewarded by becoming members of the first Sanhedrin and were given some of Moses's prophetic spirit.

Here again, it is in Rashi's assertion of his people's distinctive characteristics that his universal reach can be found. One should read his Talmudic commentaries on the creation of the first man: why was he alone? As a way of telling us, for all time and for all places, that we have one common grandfather. But Rashi doesn't mention this. Because the ethical conclusion is obvious? I will follow the example of Rashi, who admits on occasion (nearly a hundred times, in different instances) that he doesn't know.

Justice

The Talmud combines justice and charity. Let us see what Rashi says about it:

Shimon the Righteous says: the world rests on the three following things: the Torah, service to God, and deeds of loving-kindness.

Commentary: deeds of loving-kindness can be extended to the wealthy as well as to the poor, and to the dead as well as to the living; by giving money but also through actions—(but this is not justice), contrary to *tzedakah*, or almsgiving, which is an act of justice.

Rabbi Akiba says, " 'And thou shall love thy neighbor as thyself' is a great precept of the Torah." Rashi: this law applies to all men, not just to Jews.

Leadership

Toward the end of his life Moses addresses the people and sums up their common experiences: exciting moments and other less inspired ones. He also speaks of himself: "How can I myself alone bear your load, and your burden and your strife?"

Rashi: "This tells us that there *were* nonbelievers. When Moses went out early, they said: why is Amram's son going out so early? Perhaps he isn't happy at home? When he went out late, they said: why is Amram's son late? It may be that he is spending time devising bad advice for us and nursing bad thoughts about us."

(Elsewhere the Midrash tells us that Moses's situation in the camp was so unhealthy that husbands suspected him of having illicit relations with their wives.)

The eternal problem of leaders: even the peerless Moses is not above suspicion.

The Torah says: "Do not learn the abominations of the other nations."

Rashi: but understand these practices and guard against them.

After the dark episode of the Golden Calf, God says to Moses: "Go, get thee down; for thy people, which thou broughtest out of the land of Egypt, have corrupted themselves."

Rashi, to protect the people, puts the blame on the *erev rav*, the others, who joined Moses in order to leave the land of slavery. "Thy people have corrupted themselves" means: God is not speaking of *the* people but of *a* people: the others whom you converted on your own without consulting me, saying to yourself, it's good that they're in the *Shekhinah*, and now they have corrupted themselves and corrupted others.

Even the greatest leader needs God's words to inspire his own.

Responsa

Recognized as a quasi-ultimate authority, Rashi received many queries from people near and far, from disciples and peers, dealing with individual and collective problems. Hence the weight and range of his answers (over four hundred, though several may be falsely attributed to him). His opening remarks are usually personal, inquiring after the health of his correspondents and their families. He often uses the expression "in my humble opinion" or "as I was told from on high." This might not, to modern ears, sound like modesty, but it in fact presents him as nothing but a conduit for divine insight. His genuine humility never fails to inform everything he writes.

The questions—a wide spectrum—come to him from individuals, community leaders, and rabbis, living both close and far away. In some instances, says Rashi, before making a decision that will affect all its members, the community should gather in a plenary session, in absolute secrecy, in a cave. He cosigned a decision, at least once, with one Zerach ben Abraham. Rashi rarely focuses his attention on money matters. But he is attentive to the problems of individuals. A woman to whom a countess gives the order of following her on horseback asks Rashi what to do if this falls on the day of the Fast of Esther: can she put off fasting to the next day, in other words, to the day of Purim? No, says Rashi, she cannot.

The range of his answers includes problems dealing with prayer, holidays, mourning, divorce, marriage, circumcision, and the biblical and Talmudic texts.

What concerns him most is the fate of the community, tradition, ritual, the Laws, their implications and applications. Respect for his Teachers (particularly Rabbi Yaakov ben Yakar) and ancestors, the *Kadmonim*, was a determining factor for him when he ruled on the subject of the Sabbath, or the kashrut of meat or wine; he usually adopts a moderate attitude. For him, the Law isn't impersonal and shouldn't be. It involves human beings and therefore the human level should always be taken into account.

From time to time, in a difficult situation, he queried one of his teachers. Sometimes he wrote to Mainz or Worms to request clarifications of particular biblical or Talmudic interpretations based on their ancient manuscripts.

The following text, copied by Rashi himself, hardly exemplary, deals with rulings intended for his own community:

We the residents of Troyes and of the surrounding communities have ordered by oath, excommunication and strict ordinance, to all the men and women who live here, as follows:

No person can free himself of the public yoke, either today or tomorrow, with the help of the count or his representatives, who make Jews leave and separate them from the assembly of Israel. If it turns out he has not paid the tax with his brothers, we order that he will pay the same amount as each of them and that his tax will not be reduced. If he must pay the count and the latter has separated him from his brothers, from that day on he will be counted among them, and each one will pay based on his capital, based on what we the residents of the city decided and such as it has been since its inception.

The ancients who came before us passed down to us the following rules: each person will pay according to his fortune, not counting his utensils, his houses, his vineyards, his fields. As for the money of the Christians (lent to the Christians) with which he earns his keep, he will pay only on the capital. However, if he received a deposit from his fellow Jew, he will pay based on the value of half the deposit for which he has the legal responsibility. If he has silver objects, gold objects, women's jewels or rings, he will pay according to their value. If a Jew is in possession of a loan for which he is entirely responsible, such as a charitable gift that was charity for one year before becoming a loan, he will pay based on the whole amount, but during the first year.

We have also heard that such was the custom of the ancients: in cases where a city resident took money out of the city, he would have to pay based on the whole amount. However, if he has come to live here, but has not yet arranged to bring over his money, he does not have to pay until he has brought it over and started trading with it. If he has already brought over his money, but it has stayed on deposit without being used, he will pay only once he starts using it.

In cases where residents from here have made a gift to their sons and their daughters and taken it out of the city, for as long as the sons will live in the city, or if they leave it temporarily and their father intends to make them return, they will participate in the public expense with that money.

In cases where one of them received books as a security for a free loan given to his brother, he will pay based on the value of the books. (Responsum no. 248)

Rashi's concern for the individual Jew is naturally matched by his concept of what makes a community vibrant and enduring, particularly in exile: the idea of remaining attached to the Law of Moses and its ancient interpreters. Their words reverberate in his. Their decisions on an immense variety of topics and situations transcend frontiers and centuries. But the most tragic case he deals with is the fate of the converted. And there we arrive at the most painful subject as far as the Jewish people in the Rhineland are concerned: the Crusades.

Liturgical Poems

Grossman and others ascribe seven liturgical poems to Rashi. Truthfully we can say with very little hesitation that they don't really reflect Rashi's greatness. His greatness is not as a poet. Other poets of his time are more admirable. But his poems must be studied so we can better value him, and even love him.

They all describe the trials Israel is going through: the torn Torah scrolls, the students and their teachers slaughtered in a bloodbath, the ransacked synagogues: on reading them one's heart is overcome with anguish and inexpressible grief.

Was this his personal reaction to the bitter ordeal of the first Crusade?

We sense this too when we read his introduction—the only introduction he ever wrote—to the Song of Songs, which Rashi believed, according to tradition, was written by King Solomon. The great scholar Dov Rappel stresses its historical, philosophical aspect. For Yehuda Rosenthal, due to its sensitivity and brilliance, it presents a spellbinding historical allegory. For Rashi the Song was written thanks to prophetic gifts.

At first glance, it is an essentially prophetic love story between the God of Israel and the people of Israel from the Exodus out of Egypt to the destruction of the Second Temple in Jerusalem. And Rashi describes this with melancholy and hope, the one as emotional, deep, and inevitable as the other.

Let us read the text:

King Solomon had foreseen, with the help of the Holy Spirit, that it was to be Israel's destiny to go from exile to exile, from disaster to disaster, and to nostalgically bemoan the time when she was God's chosen lover. She will say: "I shall return to my first husband (God) for it was better with me than now" (Hosea 2:7). The Children of Israel will remember His kindness and also their transgressions against Him. And they will remember the kindness He promised them at the end of time.

Often the prophets compare the relations between God and Israel to those existing between an angry husband and the sinful wife who betrayed him. Solomon composed the Song of Songs using that very allegory. It is a fascinating dialogue between the husband (God) who loves and continues to love his repudiated wife, and the wife, really the widow of a living husband, who waits for her husband and seeks to get close to him once again: she recalls the love of her youthful years while recognizing her misdeed.

God too is afflicted in their affliction (Isaiah 63:9), and He remembers her youthful grace, her beauty, and the endowments for which He so loved her in the past. He lets her know that she has remained in His heart and that He will find her again, for she is still His wife and He her husband.

Rashi's commentary also includes advice on how to live in exile without capitulating: by studying in the synagogues and erecting faith as a great wall; and in the worst cases, through martyrdom. As Solomon says of the dove, Rashi says: "The dove becomes attached to his loved one. And when his throat is cut, he does not flutter and wriggle but cranes his neck." And he continues: "this virtue of self-sacrifice can only astonish the other nations of the world, and lead them all to ask: in what way is your God different from the others that you are ready to be burned and crucified for Him?"

The Song of Songs, therefore, is a story written for present and future exiles, but also a moving prayer in their memory to bring them closer to Redemption.

4

Sadness and Memory

Rashi was fifty-five at the time of the first Crusade: rumors about it must have reached him. How did he react?

Let us broaden our canvas.

The eleventh and twelfth centuries were a time of political turmoil, military turbulence, and religious upheavals. Christendom and Islam pursued their religious wars by making territorial conquests. Norway, Sweden, Burgundy, Spain, France . . . too many kings wanted to reign over too many countries. The Byzantine emperor Roman III seized Syria. In Constantinople, Patriarch Michael I Cerularius was excommunicated, precipitating the schism between the Christian East and Christian West. Benedict IX, a corrupt and cruel man, was crowned pope only to be deposed and reelected. He then sold his title and office to Gregory VI who abdicated a year later. In the Islamic world the situation was hardly more commendable. Shiites and Sunnis lived in fear and with the constant desire to win supreme domination through violence. There was the victory of William the Conqueror at

Hastings and his tumultuous reign; the invasion of the Byzantine Empire by the Turks; the appearance of anti-Papists; Rome's efforts to weaken the authority of the local princes; Gregory VII's excommunication of the German king Henry IV; the latter's forced walk to Canossa in penitence; the battles among Arabs for the reconquest of Spain; the capture of Capua by Robert Guiscard's Norman troops . . .

What a century!

Before it drew to a close, Rashif ed-din Sinan founded the secret Shiite society called the *hashishiyyin*, or "assassins," whose suicidal and murderous fanaticism is still active today. Sent to the four corners of the Islamic empire, its leaders trained flawlessly efficient professional assassins whose record of achievements would make the best specialists under contract to the Mafia jealous.

And what about the Jewish world?

While the Gentiles were busily waging bitter battles and bloody wars among themselves, by and large they still found time to take their anger out on the Jews. But less so in the eleventh century. Chroniclers related no major catastrophe. The Jews in Europe and in the Holy Land lived in relative safety, which means in relative danger. In Spain, for instance, they enjoyed the fruits of the Golden Age, a time so vibrant in our collective memories. The great thinker and poet

Shmuel ha-Nagid was commander in chief of the armies of the Catholic kings; his role in the defeat of the Muslims on several battlefields has never been questioned. Shlomo Ibn Gabirol and Yehuda ha-Levi paved the way for Maimonides. . . . The prevailing sentiment must have been, "Let's hope it lasts!" Well it didn't last. For the Jews of Western Europe the century ended in a deluge of blood, fire, and death, all in the name of a man who was born Jewish of Jewish parents, whose beautiful dream was to bring love into the hearts and souls of believers.

The Crusades. We have returned to the topic.

Don't be surprised, reader; we are not drifting away from our main subject. The Crusades concern Rashi.

It is impossible to read or reread the blunt and detailed chronicles of the period without feeling a broken heart and being overcome with despair.

It all started in Clermont-Ferrand on November 27, 1095, when Pope Urban II appealed to the Christians to go to Jerusalem and use force to liberate Christ's tomb and all the holy shrines then under Muslim rule.

Initially, the undertaking was directed against Muslims alone. The Jews were not to be affected. But some members of the French Jewish community had forebodings. Based on what? We don't know; all we know is they sent emissaries to their relatives and friends in Mainz and Worms advising them to prepare themselves for riots. Strangely incredulous, too confident, the Jews of Mainz and Worms sent the messengers away, with their messages, back to the Jews of France. Yet the French were right. When they started their crusade down the Rhine and the Danube, the Crusaders, blind with hatred, inflicted suffering and agony on the thousands upon thousands of Jews living in Cologne, Mainz, Worms, and Speyer who refused to convert to Christianity.

In some places, the Crusaders met with Jewish resistance; in others, the majority of Jews chose martyrdom. The first martyr, a woman, refused to be baptized and chose to die voluntarily. A great many coreligionists followed her example. The story of their behavior is unbearable to read. In synagogue courtyards, men recited blessings and prayers and then stabbed their wives and children to death. "Accept baptism and you will live," shouted the Crusaders wherever they suddenly appeared, like ghosts in a blaze of violence and horror. "We believe in God, in our one God," replied the Jews before dying. In some chronicles it is reported that the Crusaders entertained themselves by slashing open the bellies of pregnant women, putting live cats inside, and sewing them up.

In his masterly book on the *Akedah*, the binding of Isaac, in Jewish history, the great scholar and teacher Shalom Spiegel quotes a passage in Rabbi Eliezer bar Nathan's chronicle on the disasters of 1096. When the Crusaders entered Mehr, a village on the banks of the Rhine, the local lord delivered his Jews to them. Threatened with ugly humiliation, torture, and death, some Jews let themselves be baptized. Others were slaughtered. One man called Shmaya bribed an official who helped him escape with his wife and three sons. Then the official betrayed them. At night Shmaya slit the throats of his wife and their three children and plunged the knife into his own chest. He lost consciousness, but did not die. The next day, when the Crusaders found him lying on the ground, they said to him, "Convert to our faith and you shall live." But he answered, "May heaven protect me from renouncing the living God!" So the villagers dug a grave. The saintly Shmaya placed his wife on one side and his three sons on the other, and lay down in the middle. And the mob began to throw earth on their bodies. He was covered with earth but was still alive. They took him out. "Confess your sins and you shall live," they said to him. He refused. They put him back in the grave, but he was still alive. They took him back out again. "Are you ready to abandon your God?" The holy man, in his last breath, refused to exchange what was great and eternal for what was not. . . . He passed the test, as had Abraham the father, in bygone days! Oh, Blessed be He . . .

Why did so many men and women in the Rhine provinces choose martyrdom through suicide whereas their brothers and sisters in the Sephardic countries reacted differently? Is this due to a different mentality or to a different interpretation of the Law? Gershon Cohen published a remarkable essay on the subject. But this is not the topic at hand. The Crusades are.

When the Crusaders, led by Godfrey of Bouillon, swept into Jerusalem, they devastated the City of God and brutalized its inhabitants. Jews and Muslims combined forces and put up a courageous and relentless resistance, but they were outnumbered. The Crusaders locked up a group of Karaites in a synagogue and set it on fire. The entire group was burned alive.

Litanies and lamentations were composed describing the barbarity of the murderous invaders and the deaths of their victims. They are still recited today, on appropriate dates.

Did Rashi know what was happening in those distant lands? Word must have reached him. What does he say on the subject?

As mentioned earlier, when the first Crusade began, Rashi was fifty-five years old. He would live another ten years. He worked more, and better, than usual. His creativity was boundless. Pamphlets, halakhic decisions, new commentaries, the revision of earlier ones: he surpassed himself.

But how was this possible psychologically? How had he managed not to see, hear, or know what was going on so close to his own city? Were his powers of concentration so great and sustained? Admittedly, for incomprehensible reasons, neither his family nor his community suffered. Oddly,

Troyes was miraculously spared. But Mainz and Worms, two cities he knew well for having spent years there with his mentors, were not far away; travelers and messengers went back and forth regularly. Rashi must have had reports, if only scant ones, of the bloodbaths that had taken place in those cities. Proof: in his commentary on the Psalms, one senses his inability to hide or contain his anguish. Of course, technically, he is commenting on ancient, biblical times, but we can guess that he is actually describing his own times.

In some of his litanies of penitence, he implores God to collect the tears of children in His chalice. And he implores the holy Torah to intercede up high in favor of those who give up their lives for His glory.

Are these remarks related to the tragic events that were then unfolding in so many communities on the banks of the Rhine and far away, in Palestine?

Is his beautiful introduction (unique in its kind) to the Song of Songs a response—his response—to the pain and misfortune that have befallen his people? It expresses a stirring, very moving appeal. His aim: to bring consolation and hope to the persecuted. He says: "This song has often been commented on in the Midrashic sources, but I say that King Solomon had foreseen the time when the Children of Israel would be deported from one exile to another, from one disaster to another. And that they would lament, while recalling their past glory and the love that made them different from others. And they will remember the promises made by

God." And, Rashi adds, citing the prophets, "God will reassure them, saying that He too remembers the promises, and that their marriage is still valid: He did not send them away, Israel is still His wife and He will return to her."

Let us recall that for centuries, the faith of the Jewish people had been subjected to harsh trials in many lands. But never before with the same forceful cruelty as in Rashi's century. There were powerful elements within Christendom for whom the conversion of the Jews represented a supreme duty.

The Crusades did not come about suddenly like a clap of thunder. The groundwork had been laid by a social and religious anti-Semitism, by a noxious and sometimes lethal poison that bides its time and then strikes.

Usually the Jews resisted temptations and threats. But there were exceptions: voluntary conversions.

Rashi had to answer a question concerning a converted man who chose to return to the Jewish faith: what was the proper attitude to have toward him?

In fact, the Troyes community had already raised this problem much earlier in a letter to Rabbenu Gershom, the Light of Exile. A man who had converted voluntarily, a Cohen—hence a descendant from the line of Aaron—repented. Should he be allowed to take up his previous life? Could tradition be followed and could he be summoned to read the Torah before the others? The Cohens also have the task of blessing the assembly. Should this man be allowed to do so?

Rabbenu Gershom's answer was positive in both cases. His argument, of a general character, is simple and human. He is against any discrimination or humiliation of the reformed man and his family if he was coerced into convert-ing. (This happened to his very own son.) Worse: whoever reminds him of his baptism will be banished forever. Having recovered his rights as a Jew, all the biblical and Talmudic laws are applicable; they must be protected and respected. But if he converted voluntarily, not under duress, from inner conviction, he will be treated more harshly. By choosing apostasy in good conscience he excluded himself from the community of Israel. And then, having become an example, he will have crossed the point of no return.

Let us not forget: the number of forced and voluntary conversions at the time was very great. The spiritual leaders were duty-bound to remedy the situation by helping only the former to return, reintegrate into their communities, take their place in it, submit to their obligations, and recon-quer their rights. After all, doesn't the Talmud state that a Jew, even one who is at fault and a sinner, remains a Jew?

Rashi adopted the same line. Was it because of the Cru-sades, which, for the past six years, led to the shedding of Jewish blood wherever they appeared, with the sound and fury of unleashed fanaticism?

Rashi, whose leniency toward the victims was without bounds, does everything possible to safeguard their Jewish faith, even if secrecy has to be maintained temporarily.

He asks why galbanum, with its bad odor, was added to the incense of the Temple in Jerusalem? In order to teach us that even sinners belong to the community of Israel: together, their common prayers rise to heaven. The repentant transgressor is our brother. God is the God of us all. And we are His people.

We are back to our initial theme. *Amar Rabbi Yitzhak*, Rabbi Yitzhak says: why does the Torah start with the story of the genesis of the world rather than the first law?

This is better understood if we place Rashi's oeuvre and thought in its historical context.

On the one hand, Rome was saying to the Jews: come to us; you are no longer God's people; we are His people. It is we who carry His word, His promise. But Rashi is entitled to say: so long as a Jew remains faithful to God, God remains faithful to him.

And on the other hand?

At the time, Christians and Muslims were at war over the ownership of a small strip of land called Palestine. Each side sacrificed their sons to possess it. So the Jew Rashi reminds them of this ancient legend:

One day the nations of the world will tell the Jews, this land is ours; you stole it from us. And we will reply: the land belongs to God; He alone has the right to say who will live there. And He gave this land to us.

As mentioned already, Rashi completed his biblical commentaries, but not his Talmudic ones. They were completed by his close disciples.

The expression *"kaan niftar rabenu,"* "here, in this spot, our Teacher died," or *"kaan hifsik rabenu,"* "here our Teacher interrupted his work," occurs three times in his commentary of the Talmud. In Tractate *Baba Batra*, the text is clear: "What preceded was Rashi's commentary; what follows is that of his grandson, Rashbam." In the Pizarro edition, the information is more explicit: "Here Rashi left this world." In Tractate Makkot (criminal punishment), the rhythm of the text is suddenly interrupted: "Our Teacher who lived and worked, pure in body and soul, ended his task here. From now on, it is Rabbi Yehuda bar Nathan who is speaking." In Tractate Pesahim (Passover), the interruption is more succinct: "This is the commentary of Rabbi Shmuel, Rashi's disciple."

It is clear: Rashi had interrupted his work several times.

Let us remember: as Professor Abraham Grossman vividly demonstrates in his work, Rashi's singular greatness was in opening "the doors and windows" of his school to all the traditions that existed in Babylon, Palestine, Italy, Germany, Provence, and Spain. Furthermore, Rashi taught his disciples to engage in open discussions including polemics with the Christian world.

In other words, he believed that scholars must not dwell in the isolation of their studies but in creative dialogue.

If one may speak of universalism in Jewish thought, it surely applies to our Master and teacher, Rabbi Shlomo ben Yitzhak of Troyes.

The last years of his life were trying. Was it because of the depressing news that came from communities not so far away? He became ill. He had difficulty writing. Often he dictated his responsa, to Rabbi Azriel or Rabbi Yosef, for instance. He said so in his letters: "I don't have the strength to hold a pen in my hand." But even in a world where, in some places, because of ancient, hate-filled, brutal reasons, Death is glorified, his message remains alive and an admirable celebration of life.

CHRONOLOGY

586 BCE   The Kingdom of Judah is defeated by the Babylonians and its leaders exiled to Babylon.

539 BCE   The Persian emperor Cyrus the Great, having defeated the Babylonian Empire, allows exiled Jews to begin to return to the Land of Israel and undertake rebuilding the Temple.

458 BCE   Ezra, a leader of Jews who has been exiled in Babylonia, returns to the land of Israel with his followers. Also institutes the practice of publicly reading the Torah in synagogue.

c. 300–250 BCE   Emergence of the Septuagint, the Greek translation of the Bible, composed for the benefit of Greek-speaking Jews in Alexandria.

70 CE   The Roman emperor Titus crushes the Jewish revolt in Jerusalem, destroying

the Temple. Jews are sent into exile throughout the Roman Empire, some as far as France; the rabbinic leadership reconvenes in the city of Yavneh in northern Israel, where they establish their academy.

ca. 77   Flavius Josephus, a Jewish historian and commander in the war against Rome who, after his capture by the Romans, became a favorite of the emperor, writes *The Jewish War*, his history of the war against Rome.

ca. 100   Onkelos, a proselyte and contemporary of the Rabban Gamliel and Eliezer ben Hyracnus, prominent rabbis of the Mishnah, translates the Bible into Aramaic, the common language of Jews at that time. Onkelos's Aramaic translation, which by necessity contains interpretation, is still printed as one of the standard commentaries on the Torah.

ca. 200   Rabbi Judah ha-Nasi codifies the Mishnah, a collection of Jewish Law derived from the Torah.

928   Saadiah ben Joseph, an Egyptian-born scholar then living in Babylonia, appointed head or *gaon* of the Talmud academy in Sura, Babylonia, one of the two cities which were then the centers of Jewish scholarship. He was the creator of rabbinic literature, author of important works on *halakhah*, as well as one of the first Jewish philosophers. He also translated the Bible into Arabic, and was an important compiler of liturgy and author of *piyyutim* (liturgical poems).

ca. 950   Birth of Shimon bar Yitzhak, one of the earliest German authors of liturgical poems, colleague of Rabbenu Gershom, the famed German rabbi and leader of Western European Jewry, and uncle of Rashi.

ca. 950–960   Menahem ben Jacon ibn Saruq, Spanish author and lexicographer, writes *Mahberet*, a Hebrew-language dictionary of Hebrew and Aramaic; it is used by scholars throughout Europe.

ca. 960   Dunash ben Labrat, a Hebrew poet and lexicographer, attacks ibn Saruq's

Mahberet on the grounds that some of its definitions may lead to heresy; the controversy continues for generations, well into the time of Rashi and his descendants.

ca. 11th century Rabbi Yosef bar Shmuel Tov-elem Bonfils, born in Narbonne, France. An author of *piyyutim* and influential halakhic decisions, he is the first French rabbi who can be identified beyond his name.

1012 Jews briefly expelled from Mainz.

ca. 1021 Birth of Solomon ben Judah ibn Gabirol, great Spanish philosopher and author of both religious and secular poetry.

1028 Death of Rabbenu Gershom ben Judah Meor ha-Golah, in Mainz. Rabbenu Gershom's most famous decisions, prohibiting polygamy and the reading of private letters, are known throughout the Ashkenazic world. Rabbenu Gershom's students, Rabbi Yitzhak ben Yehuda and Rabbi Yaakov ben Yakar, who will be Rashi's teachers, take over the yeshiva.

1038 Shmuel ha-Nagid, the halakhist and leader of Spanish Jewry, becomes vizier of Granada, then under Muslim rule.

1040 Solomon ben Isaac, later known as Rashi, born in Troyes, France.

1064 Death of Rashi's favorite teacher, Rabbi Yaakov ben Yakar, who had been a disciple of Rabbenu Gershom. In Rashi's commentaries he is identified as "my teacher in Scripture."

ca. 1070 Rashi founds a school in Troyes.

ca. 1089 Birth of Abraham ben Meir ibn Ezra, in Tudela, Spain. Ibn Ezra will go on to become one of the most significant Hebrew poets and biblical commentators, a major proponent of the *peshat* school of exegesis.

1095 Pope Urban II preaches that Christian soldiers should retake Jerusalem from the Muslims, initiating what will be the First Crusade. Christian soldiers set off for the Holy Land, massacring Jews in France, the Rhineland, and Bohemia along the way.

1099 Crusader Godfrey of Boullon conquers Jerusalem, massacring Jews and Karaites.

1105 Rashi dies. His grandson and disciple Shmuel ben Meir, known as the Rashbam, one of the most prominent Tosafists, completes Rashi's commentary on several tractates of the Talmud.

1138 Birth of Moses ben Maimon, known as Maimonides or Rambam, the great Spanish philosopher, commentator, writer, and codifier of *halakhah* and physician to Saladin, as well as *nagid*, leader, of all Jews under Saladin's empire.

1141 Death of Judah ha-Levi, the great Hebrew poet, philosopher, and friend of Abraham ibn Ezra. Born in Spain, he died in the land of Israel.

1144 The first blood libel takes place in Norwich, England.

1146 The passage of the Second Crusade through France causes one of Rashi's

grandsons, Jacob ben Meir, known as
Rabbenu Tam, to leave his home in
Ramerupt, France. The greatest scholar
of his generation, Rabbenu Tam wrote
extensive responsa as well as Hebrew
poetry and grammar.

1150   Rabbi Eliezer bar Nathan of Mainz, a
leading German rabbinical authority,
together with Rabbenu Tam and
Rashbam, composes *Takkanot Troyes*, the
Ordinance of Troyes, the directives
governing the Jews of that community.

1190   Saladin reconquers Jerusalem from the
Crusaders, permits Jewish resettlement.

1194   Birth in Spain of Moses ben Nachman,
known as Nachmanides or Ramban, a
major philosopher, Talmudist, and
Kabbalist whose biblical commentary
appears in the standard texts with that
of Rashi. His teachers were trained by
the Tosafists of northern France, the
school of Rashi's disciples.

ca. 1205–1218   The Radak, Rabbi David Kimhi, a
grammarian and exegete in Narbonne,

France, participates in the judgment of several men from Barcelona who dishonored Rashi's memory.

1288 A blood libel in Troyes leads to the execution of thirteen Jews, inspiring laments by the Hebrew-French poet Jacob ben Judah of Lorraine, who witnessed the event.

1322 Nicholas de Lyre, a Christian biblical commentator and theologian, begins to publish his *Postillae Perpetuae*, the first Christian Bible commentary to be printed. He relies heavily on Rashi, whom he also translated into Latin.

ca. 1470 Birth of Obadiah ben Jacob Sforno, a major Italian biblical commentator.

1475 First known printed Hebrew book is produced in Italy. A Bible with Rashi's commentary, it uses a cursive script typeface for Rashi's comments, a typeface that will come to be known as "Rashi script."

1503 Don Isaac Abrabanel, a Portuguese-born financier and biblical exegete who had fled Portugal and Spain rather than convert to Christianity, settles in Venice where he will continue to write his commentaries on the Bible.

1517 Daniel Bomberg, a Christian printer of Hebrew books, publishes *Mikra'ot Gedolot*, a Hebrew Torah with commentary by Rashi, ibn Ezra, and others. Establishes the convention of printing the commentaries in "Rashi script." He goes on to publish the Talmud, also with commentaries in Rashi script, including those of Rashi and his grandsons, the Tosafists.

1614 Rabbi Yom Tov Lipmann ha-Levi Heller, a purported descendant of Rashi, begins to publish his commentary on the Mishnah, the *Tosafot Yom Tov*.

1649 Rabbi Isaiah ben Abraham ha-Levi Horowitz, a purported descendant of Rashi, publishes his *Shnei Luchot ha-Brit*, a guide to ethical life combining *halakhah*, kabbalah, and moral instruction.

ca. 1735   Israel ben Eliezer, known as the Ba'al Shem Tov, founds the Hasidic movement, which stresses ecstatic prayer and mysticism. His influence soon spreads among the Jews of Eastern Europe.

1772   Birth of Nahman of Bratzlav, who will go on to be a major Hasidic thinker.

1791   Emancipation of the Jews of France.

1895   Albert Dreyfus, a Jewish captain on the French Army General Staff, is convicted of treason and publicly demoted on a tide of French anti-Semitism. He was exonerated in 1906.

June 1940   France surrenders to the German army. The country is divided into two zones; the north is under direct German control, and the south is ruled by a French puppet government based in Vichy.

November 1942   Germans take control of all of France. Deportations of Jews increase. More than eighty thousand Jews from France, both native French and Jewish immigrants to France, are killed at Auschwitz by the end of the war. Many more Jews suffer greatly in work camps and forced labor battalions.

May 14, 1948 Founding of the State of Israel.

1989 Rashi Institute, dedicated to Jewish scholarship, opens in Troyes.

GLOSSARY

Aramaic   A Semitic language, related to Hebrew and Arabic, which flourished in the Mesopotamian world in different forms from approximately 700 BCE to the middle of the first millennium CE, and is still spoken by small groups in Lebanon, Turkey, and Kurdistan. The language of the Talmud and other important Jewish texts, Aramaic was used for rabbinic writings through the thirteenth century CE.

Ashkenazi   Originally referred to Jews from Germany; eventually generalized to include all Jews from Central and Eastern Europe.

Belaaz   From the Hebrew *be*, "in," and *lo'ez*, "foreign." *Laaz* eventually came to be associated with Romance languages, so the term *belaaz* is used to introduce a translation from Hebrew into one of those languages. Frequently used by Rashi to refer to Old French.

Blood libel   The anti-Jewish slander, first appearing in Norwich, England, in 1144, that Jews kill Christian children and use their blood for ritual purposes, especially on Passover. This slander occasionally still surfaces and has been the pretext for anti-Jewish violence over the centuries, leading to much death and destruction.

Diaspora   The Jewish communities outside the land of Israel. After the destruction of the Jerusalem Temple in the year 70 CE, most Jews were exiled from the land of Israel, but they never ceased to long to return to the land.

Drash   One of the four traditional methods of exegesis, referring to an interpretive commentary on a biblical verse.

Gaonic period   From the end of the sixth through the middle of the eleventh century, the period during which the *geonim*, the leaders of the yeshivas of Sura and Pumpedita in Babylonia, were the accepted legal authorities of the Jewish world.

Mahzor Vitry   A guide to liturgy and *halakhah* written by Rashi's student, Simhah ben Shmuel of Vitry. *Mahzor Vitry* is based on Rashi's halakhic rulings for the liturgy of the entire cycle of holidays, including Shabbat, and is also a valuable record of Jewish life in France in Rashi's time.

Mainz   A city on the Rhine River in Germany, capital of the Rhineland region and site of Jewish settlement from at least the mid-tenth century. Mainz is 282 miles northeast of Troyes.

Midrash   A method of exegesis of biblical texts; a legal, exegetical, or homiletical commentary on the Bible. Also refers to the collections thereof.

Mishnah   The collection of rabbinic legal opinions redacted by Rabbi Judah ha-Nasi, around the year 220. The Mishnah is the primary text of Jewish law or *halakhah*. It is divided into six orders, *sedarim*, which are further divided into sixty-three tractates.

Mitzvot   Hebrew for commandments (singular is mitzvah), referring to God's commandments. Used colloquially to refer to "good deeds."

Peshat   One of the four traditional methods of biblical exegesis, focusing on the simple or literal meaning of the text. This was Rashi's preferred means of explanation.

Remez   One of the four traditional methods of biblical exegesis, focusing on the allusive level of meaning.

Responsa   The term for the continually evolving body of Jewish legal decisions developed as responses to questions posed to rabbis.

Sefer Torah   The scroll of the Five Books of Moses (Pentateuch), read in synagogue.

Shekhinah   The Divine presence. *Shekhinah*, which is a feminine noun, often refers to the feminine attributes of God.

Sod   One of the four traditional methods of biblical exegesis, referring to the mystical meaning of the text.

Talmud   A collection of rabbinic legal rulings and teachings compiled in the fifth century. The Talmud comprises the Mishnah, the rabbinic opinions codified at the beginning of the third century by Rabbi Judah the Prince, and the Gemara, which is a rabbinic interpretation of the

Mishnah as well as a host of other discussions, from the third through fifth centuries. Rabbinic academies in Babylonia and in Israel developed their own Talmuds; the Babylonian Talmud is generally considered more authoritative than the Jerusalem Talmud. The central text of Jewish law, the Talmud is usually printed accompanied by later commentaries, including Rashi's.

Torah   The Five Books of Moses, also called the Pentateuch, comprising the first section of the Hebrew Bible. Also used more generally to refer to Jewish learning and Jewish texts.

Tosafists   The scholars of the generations after Rashi, including his sons-in-law and grandsons. These rabbis composed the *Tosafot* (literally, "additional") commentaries on the Talmud, as well as many important halakhic works.

Tosefta   A collection of rabbinic opinions from the period of the Mishnah that were not included in the Mishnah.

Tractate   The sixty-three subdivisions of the six orders, or main sections, of the Mishnah. Not all of these tractates have a corresponding expansion into the Gemara.

Trop   The musical cantillation used for chanting of biblical texts in the synagogue.

Troyes   The home of Rashi, a city in the Champagne region of France, 118 miles southeast of Paris.

Worms   A city in the Rhineland region of Germany, about

twenty-eight miles south of Mainz. Jews had settled in Worms by the end of the tenth century.

Yeshiva   An academy of Jewish learning. From the Hebrew word for "sit," the yeshiva is named for the practice of sitting and studying, primarily the Talmud.

BIBLIOGRAPHY

Catane, Moshe (Paul Klein). *La vie en France au XIe siècle d'après les écrits de Rachi*. Jerusalem: Gallia, 1994.

Darmesteter, Arsène. *Les gloses Françaises de Rachi dans la Bible*. Paris: Librairie Durlacher, 1909.

Liber, Maurice. *Rashi*. Adele Szold, translator. New York: Dybbuk Press, LLC, 2006.

Pearl, Chaim. *Rashi*. New York: Grove Press, 1998.

Rashi Anniversary Volume. New York: American Academy of Jewish Research, 1941.

Schwarzfuchs, Simon. *Rashi de Troyes*. Paris: Albin Michel, 2005.

Sed-Rajna, Gabrielle, ed. *Rashi, 1040–1990 Hommage a Ephraim E. Urbach*. Paris: Congres Europeen des etudes Juives, 1993.

Shereshevsky, Esra. *Rashi: The Man and His World*. Lanham, Md.: Jason Aronson, 1996.

Bibliography

י"ל מימון (עורך), ספר רש"י, ירושלים, תשט"ז

ש' פדרבוש (עורך), רש"י: תורתו ואישיותו, ניו יורק, תשי"ח

צ"א שטיינפלד, רש"י: עיונים ביצירתו, רמת גן, תשנ"ג

י' בער, "רש"י והמציאות ההיסטורית של זמנו", תרביץ, כ(תש"ט), עמ' 320-332

א' ברלינר, "לתולדות פירושי רש"י", כתבים נבחרים, ב, ירושלים, תש"ט, עמ' 226-279

א' גרוסמן, חכמי צרפת הראשונים, ירושלים, תשמ"ט

א' גרוסמן, רש"י, ירושלים, תשס"ו

נ' ליבוביץ ומ' ארנד, פירוש רש"י לתורה: עיונים בשיטתו, האוניברסיטה הפתוחה, תל אביב, תש"ן

ש"א פוזננסקי, מבוא על חכמי צרפת מפרשי המקרא, ירושלים, תשכ"ה

מ' קטן, אוצר לעזי רש"י, ירושלים, תשמ"ד

מ' קטן, החיים בימי רש"י, ירושלים, תשנ"ז

ש' קמין, רש"י: פשוטו של מקרא ומדרשו של מקרא, ירושלים, תשמ"ו

י' רחמן, אגדת רש"י, תל אביב, 1991

ד' רפל, רש"י: תמונת עולמו היהודית, ירושלים, תשנ"ה

ש' שוורצפוקס, יהודי צרפת בימי הביניים, תל אביב, 2001

י"מ תא-שמע, הספרות הפרשנית לתלמוד באירופה ובצפון אפריקה, א, ירושלים, תשנ"ט

ABOUT THE AUTHOR

Elie Wiesel is the author of more than fifty books, both fiction and nonfiction, including his masterly memoir *Night*. He has been awarded the United States Congressional Gold Medal of Achievement, the Presidential Medal of Freedom, the rank of Grand-Croix in the French Legion of Honor, an honorary knighthood of the British Empire, and, in 1986, the Nobel Peace Prize. Since 1976, he has been the Andrew W. Mellon Professor in the Humanities at Boston University.